It's another Quality Book from CGP

This book is for anyone doing OCR B GCSE History.

Whatever subject you're doing, it's the same old story — there are lots of facts and you've just got to learn them. GCSE History is no different.

Happily, this CGP book gives you all that important information as clearly and concisely as possible.

There's even a section to help you score full marks for your spelling, punctuation and grammar.

What CGP is all about

Our sole aim here at CGP is to produce the highest quality books — carefully written, immaculately presented, and dangerously close to being funny.

Then we work our socks off to get them out to you — at the cheapest possible prices.

CONTENTS

PART ONE: INTERNATIONAL RELATIONS

PART TWO: DEPTH STUDIES

PART TWO CONTINUED...

Section 7 — Causes and Events of the First World War

Section 8 — The USA 1945-1975

PART THREE: BRITISH DEPTH STUDY

✱ Section 9 — Changes in British Society, 1890-1918

Exam Advice

We've included the most popular options for OCR B GCSE History — you'll need to check with your teacher which topics you should revise for your exams.

Published by CGP

Editors:

Heather Gregson, Anthony Muller, Luke von Kotze

Contributors:

David Barnes, Rene Cochlin, Robert Gibson, John O'Malley, John Pritchard

With thanks to Claire Boulter and Vanessa Musgrove for the proofreading.

ISBN: 978 1 84762 412 3

Clipart from Corel®
Printed by Elanders Ltd, Newcastle upon Tyne.
Based on the classic CGP style created by Richard Parsons.
Coordinated by Paddy Gannon.

The Peace Settlement

World War One lasted from <u>1914-1918</u>. Fighting ended with the armistice on November 11th 1918. The allies (Britain, France and the USA) won. They then had to agree a <u>peace treaty</u> with the losers — including Germany.

There were Three Concerns to think about

1) <u>Millions</u> of people were <u>dead</u> or <u>injured</u>. Countries like Belgium and France were <u>devastated</u> — the main powers had <u>spent too much</u> money on the war.

2) Many people wanted Germany to take all the <u>blame</u>, especially in Britain and France — so Germany and its allies <u>weren't allowed</u> to take part in the talks.

3) Everyone wanted to make sure a war like this <u>wouldn't happen again</u>, but they <u>couldn't agree</u> on how to do this — the system of alliances had obviously <u>failed</u>.

The Big Three were France, Britain and the USA

1) All three countries had ideas about the settlement, and they often <u>disagreed</u>.

2) So a <u>compromise</u> was reached — only some of their ideas became part of the settlement.

3) The key fact to remember is that the French had <u>suffered badly</u>, and the British had <u>also suffered</u> — this meant they both wanted to <u>punish</u> the Germans. But people in the USA had <u>suffered less</u> — so they were less emotional and wanted to stay <u>impartial</u>.

Georges Clemenceau
French PM

David Lloyd George
British PM

Woodrow Wilson
US President

Wilson suggested 14 Points

1) President Wilson had come up with the <u>Fourteen Points</u> in January 1918 when the Germans were asking for a truce.

2) Germany <u>rejected</u> them then, but when the fighting ended they changed their minds and wanted to base the <u>peace settlement</u> on them.

3) The Allies <u>refused</u> Wilson's Points because the Germans had rejected them before.

4) But the Fourteen Points were an important part of the <u>peace process</u> — especially point 14 which called for a <u>League of Nations</u> to settle disputes. This was going to become very important between the two world wars.

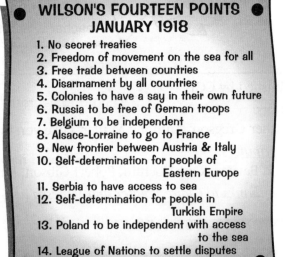

**WILSON'S FOURTEEN POINTS
JANUARY 1918**

1. No secret treaties
2. Freedom of movement on the sea for all
3. Free trade between countries
4. Disarmament by all countries
5. Colonies to have a say in their own future
6. Russia to be free of German troops
7. Belgium to be independent
8. Alsace-Lorraine to go to France
9. New frontier between Austria & Italy
10. Self-determination for people of Eastern Europe
11. Serbia to have access to sea
12. Self-determination for people in Turkish Empire
13. Poland to be independent with access to the sea
14. League of Nations to settle disputes

The Fourteen Points — giving peace a chance...

Once the war was over you'd have thought the squabbling would stop, but instead the winners argued about what should happen next. Don't forget the reasons why Britain and France had <u>different ideas</u> from the USA. Scribble a list of the <u>Fourteen Points</u> and get it learned.

The Versailles Treaty

Wilson's Fourteen Points would have been pretty good for the Germans — but things didn't work out that way. After a lot of negotiating, the <u>reality</u> was the Treaty of Versailles.

The <u>Treaty of Versailles</u> was signed in June 1919

1) This treaty (agreement) dealt with <u>Germany</u>, but the other defeated countries made <u>separate treaties</u>.
2) This map shows the <u>key changes</u>, so go around it carefully and make sure you know who got what.
3) Start by looking at the land Germany <u>lost</u> — especially Alsace and Lorraine (A), the large piece of land to the west of Germany.
4) The <u>Rhineland</u> (R) was <u>demilitarised</u> — Germany <u>wasn't allowed</u> to have troops there as it was close enough to invade France and Belgium from.
5) Look at the <u>new countries</u> set up, particularly the ones near Germany. Some contained many different nationalities within their borders. They were potentially <u>unstable</u>.

Countries made from the Turkish Empire
Countries made from Austria-Hungary
Countries made from the Russian Empire
Land taken from Germany
Demilitarised Zone

THE SETTLEMENT AFTER THE FIRST WORLD WAR

The <u>Results</u> of the <u>Versailles Treaty</u> were <u>Severe</u>

1) It wasn't just land that Germany lost. Article 231 of the treaty said Germany had to take the <u>blame</u> for the war — the <u>War-Guilt Clause</u>.
2) Germany's armed forces were <u>reduced</u> to 100 000 men, only volunteers, without armoured vehicles, aircraft or submarines, and only 6 warships.
3) Germany was <u>forced to pay</u> £6600 million in reparations — payments for the damage caused. The amount was decided in 1921 but was changed later. It would have taken Germany until the 1980s to pay.
4) Germany <u>lost</u> its empire — areas around the world that used to belong to Germany were now called <u>mandates</u>, and they were going to be run by...
5) ...the <u>League of Nations</u>, which was set up to keep world peace — you're going to have to learn a lot more about this organisation.

Versailles — no treats for the Germans...

This treaty was the <u>key document</u> in Europe for the next twenty years — and it was a major cause of the <u>Second World War</u>. The Germans were very unhappy with the results of the treaty, and it would cause major problems later...

Reactions to the Treaty

A lot of people <u>didn't like</u> the Treaty of Versailles — Lloyd George and Wilson thought it wouldn't work, and Clemenceau was criticised by many French people who thought it wasn't harsh enough.

Some people said the Treaty was Fair

1) Some people thought the Treaty of Versailles was fair because the war had caused so much <u>death and damage</u>.
2) They thought <u>Germany</u> had to be <u>made weaker</u> so it couldn't go to war again.
3) People in France and Britain wanted <u>revenge</u> — politicians listened to them so that they could stay in power.

Others said the Treaty was too Harsh

1) The Germans were left <u>weak</u> and <u>resentful</u> — this could lead to <u>anger</u> and cause future trouble, like another war.
2) The treaty <u>wouldn't</u> help rebuild European <u>trade</u> and <u>wealth</u> — Germany <u>couldn't afford</u> the reparations, and many of the new countries were poor.
3) The peacemakers faced problems and <u>pressure</u> from the people at home.

Germany Hated the Treaty of Versailles

The Germans were very <u>bitter</u> about the treaty because they...

couldn't afford reparations

didn't accept guilt for starting the war

lost industrial areas and could not rebuild

suffered an economic crisis

lost pride without armed forces

lost colonies

saw other countries weren't disarming

didn't accept defeat

often now lived under foreign rule in new countries

Problems were Building up for the Future

1) Europe <u>couldn't recover</u> properly while countries like Germany remained <u>poor</u>.
2) Self-determination would be <u>difficult</u> in new countries like Poland and Czechoslovakia where many people from <u>different nationalities</u> had been <u>thrown together</u> as an artificial country.
3) German <u>anger</u> would lead to <u>trouble</u> in the future. The Germans called the treaty a '<u>Diktat</u>' — they had <u>no choice</u> about accepting it.
4) Without Germany, Russia or USA in the <u>League of Nations</u>, it'd be <u>hard</u> to keep the peace.

After the Treaty — there may be trouble ahead...

I'm afraid we've got more treaties to come — but the key here is that you understand the <u>main points and effects</u> of the Treaty of Versailles. Scribble two lists — one for the reasons some people thought the treaty was <u>too harsh</u>, and the other with the reasons some people said it was <u>fair</u>. Remember — you need to be able to give <u>both sides</u> of the case.

The Other Treaties

Versailles was really only about Germany — other treaties dealt with the rest of the losers.

Three more treaties Caused Trouble

TREATY	DEALT WITH	MAIN POINTS
ST. GERMAIN 1919	AUSTRIA	Separated Austria from Hungary. Stopped Austria joining with Germany. Took land away, e.g. Bosnia. Made Austria limit its army. Created new countries (see p.3).
TRIANON 1920	HUNGARY	Took land away, e.g. Croatia. Made Hungary reduce its army. Created new countries (see p.3).
SÈVRES 1920	TURKEY	Lost land — part of Turkey became new mandates, e.g. Syria. Turkey lost control of the Black Sea.

1) New countries like Czechoslovakia and Yugoslavia were formed out of Austria-Hungary.
2) Austria and Hungary's separation was important — and the fact that Austria wasn't allowed to join with Germany. Both Austria and Hungary suffered badly after the war.
3) The Turks hated Sèvres. Turkish nationalists like Mustafa Kemal resisted the treaty and forced some later changes — in the Treaty of Lausanne in 1923. This reduced the amount of territory to be lost by Turkey and scrapped all reparations.
4) The Arabs who fought alongside the Allies didn't gain as much as they'd hoped.

The Treaties had Similar Results

1) All the defeated countries lost land, and had to disarm.
2) They were all punished, following the pattern of Versailles.
3) Versailles, St. Germain and Trianon were the harshest treaties — Germany, Austria and Hungary lost valuable industrial land. Bulgaria wasn't so badly treated because it hadn't played such a big part in the war.
4) Countries which were created or increased because of the treaties — like Czechoslovakia, Yugoslavia and Poland — were now governing people of many different nationalities.
5) Czechoslovakia, for example, had Germans, Slovaks, Hungarians, Poles, Ukrainians, and over 6 million Czechs. Tricky one deciding what language to speak.

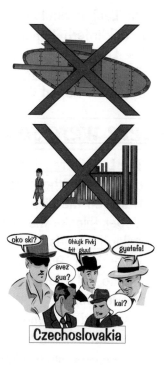

Czechoslovakia

The treaty was a charmer — so disarming...

You'd be smart to get the names of the treaties and the countries involved all learned now. Learn the five key results of the treaties and the patterns that show how they all followed the example of Versailles. The new countries were artificial — and would cause big problems later.

The League of Nations

There were high hopes for the League of Nations. Lots of people admired its moral principles.

The League came from the Fourteen Points

The Assembly
Met once a year. Each country had 1 vote. Could only recommend to council.

Stop Aggression

Encourage Cooperation

The Council
Met about 3 times per year, or in emergency. 5 permanent members - Br, Fr, It, Jap, Ger (mem. 1926). Also had temporary members.

Disarmament

Improve living and working conditions

Secretariat
Carried out the work of the League, like a civil service.

Special Commissions
e.g. Mandates, Refugees, Slavery, Health Organisation

International Labour Organisation
Worked to improve working conditions

Permanent Court of International Justice

The flags show the four main aims of the League.

The rest of the diagram shows how the League was organised and which parts of the organisation were responsible for what.

KEY: Br = Britain,
Fr = France, It = Italy,
Jap = Japan, Ger = Germany

The League was intended to Police the World

1) It began work in January 1920.
2) There were 42 members to start with, and around 60 by the 1930s.
3) All the members followed a Covenant (agreement) of 26 rules.
4) Every member country had a vote in the Assembly and the Council.
5) The League could warn countries in disputes, apply economic sanctions (block international trade with misbehaving countries), then send troops in.
6) The League tried to improve social conditions, working on health, slavery and refugees.
7) The Permanent International Court of Justice decided on border disputes between countries. Everyone hoped this would avoid another major war.

There were some early Successes

1) The League resolved several difficult situations over territorial claims — without fighting.
2) It solved the dispute in 1921 between Germany and Poland over Upper Silesia, the dispute between Sweden and Finland over the Aaland Islands in 1921, and the conflict when Greece invaded Bulgaria in 1925. These successes gave it a good reputation.
3) It also did a lot of good work to help refugees after the First World War.
4) It worked to combat the spread of serious diseases such as leprosy, malaria and plague — and inoculated against them.
5) It fought against slavery, and tried to create better working conditions for people all across the world.

Policing the nations — in a league of its own...

The main thing you need to know here is how the League was supposed to work, its main aims, and some examples of its early successes.

Problems with the League of Nations

From the start, the League of Nations had real problems.

The USA Didn't Join the League

Wilson was very ill by this time, and Congress rejected the League.
The USA never became a member. Learn these reasons why:

1) The people of America hadn't liked the Versailles treaty, and refused to accept it. They thought the League of Nations was connected to it.
2) They believed it would be too expensive — many people wanted to stay out of Europe, and wanted only to worry about American affairs. This attitude was called isolationism.
3) Many thought that all people should be free under democracy. They weren't willing to be dragged into wars to help countries like Britain and France keep undemocratic colonies.
4) Wilson's political enemies wanted to make him unpopular, and get rid of him.

The League Wasn't Powerful Enough

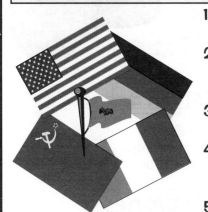

1) Britain and France were in charge, but neither country was strong enough after the war to do the job properly.
2) Economic and military sanctions could only work if a powerful nation like the USA was applying them. Most countries were too busy rebuilding to be able to apply them.
3) Germany and communist Russia were not allowed to be members when the League was first formed.
4) The League had no army of its own, and most members didn't want to commit troops to war. Some countries like Italy were quite prepared to ignore the League.
5) The organisation was a disaster — in the Assembly and the Council everyone had to agree before anything could happen. The Court of Justice had no powers to make a country act.

Two Conflicts caused the League Problems in 1923

THE CORFU INCIDENT

1) The Italian leader Mussolini occupied the Greek island of Corfu in 1923 after the murder of an Italian diplomat.
2) Mussolini demanded financial compensation and an apology from Greece.
3) The League demanded that the money should be paid to them, not Italy.
4) But Mussolini got the decision overturned and received the money and the apology he wanted. The League looked weak.

FRENCH OCCUPATION OF THE RUHR

1) Germany failed to keep up with its reparation payments.
2) In retaliation, France invaded and occupied an industrial region of Germany called the Ruhr in 1923.
3) The League of Nations didn't intervene.
4) The United States helped resolve the situation with the Dawes Plan (see p.36).
5) France withdrew from the Ruhr in 1925.

Big problems — hardly the Premier League...

The League was doomed from the start, I'm afraid — but you need to be able to argue for the good and the bad sides of the League. The biggest problem it had was when the USA didn't join — even though the idea had come from the US President in the first place.

The Effects of the Great Depression

One of the things that really <u>undermined</u> the <u>League of Nations</u> was the <u>Great Depression</u>...

The American Stock Market Crashed in 1929

1) In the 1920s, the USA was the <u>most prosperous</u> country in the world, with <u>high wages</u> and <u>mass production</u> of goods. The '<u>Booming Twenties</u>' saw billions of dollars <u>loaned</u> by the USA to help European countries <u>recover</u> from the effects of the First World War. American companies were <u>selling</u> lots of goods, so people <u>borrowed</u> money to <u>buy shares</u> in them.

2) But <u>problems</u> started to emerge. Many American producers <u>overproduced</u> — there was too much <u>supply</u> and not enough <u>demand</u>. There was <u>competition</u> from countries like Japan.

3) In <u>1929</u>, the American <u>stock market crashed</u> — people realised some companies were doing badly and rushed to <u>sell their shares</u>.

4) <u>Wall Street</u> is the <u>financial centre</u> of the USA where <u>stocks</u> and <u>shares</u> are traded — by October 1929 the selling was <u>frantic</u>, and <u>prices</u> <u>dropped</u> because people no longer wanted to buy shares at high prices.

5) Businesses <u>collapsed</u> and thousands of people were <u>ruined</u> — by the end of the month they were selling shares for whatever they could get for them. This was the start of the <u>Great Depression</u> — a global <u>economic downturn</u>.

The Depression caused big problems in America

1) In 1929 the USA <u>stopped</u> lending money abroad and <u>called in</u> its loans.

2) By 1930 nearly 2000 banks <u>collapsed</u> as people <u>rushed</u> to <u>withdraw</u> savings.

3) Three years later there were over <u>12 million</u> people <u>unemployed</u> in the USA.

The Depression Affected other Industrial Countries

1) Most <u>industrial countries</u> were <u>affected</u> — banks failed, industries struggled, and trade ground to a halt. The <u>least affected</u> country was the USSR, which had a <u>communist</u> system.

2) Within three years there were over <u>2.5 million</u> people <u>unemployed</u> in Britain, and more than 30 million unemployed in the industrial countries of the West.

3) Germany, which had <u>relied</u> on American loans, was particularly <u>badly affected</u>, with banks failing, exports suffering and unemployment rising to over <u>6 million Germans</u> by 1932.

The Depression made the League's work more Difficult

1) The Depression caused widespread <u>poverty</u>. People were <u>more likely</u> to <u>support</u> extreme <u>right-wing leaders</u> — hoping they'd provide strong government.

2) In 1933, the <u>Nazis</u>, led by Hitler, were elected in <u>Germany</u>. The Nazis wanted to <u>defy</u> the <u>League of Nations</u> by overturning the Treaty of Versailles.

3) The Depression meant that countries like Britain and France were <u>less willing</u> to <u>help</u> the League by getting involved in resolving international conflicts. They wanted to concentrate on dealing with <u>domestic problems</u> like unemployment.

4) The Depression was also a factor in some <u>international conflicts</u>, e.g. the Manchurian Crisis (see p.9).

The Wall Street crash — a depressing subject...

The Depression didn't just affect the world economy — it affected world <u>politics</u> too.
Countries that had nearly recovered from World War One found themselves in dire straits again.

The Manchurian Crisis

On the other side of the world, <u>Japan</u> had suffered badly during the <u>Depression</u>.

The USA saw Japan as a Threat

1) Japan had been at <u>war</u> with Russia in 1904.
2) Japanese industries had <u>grown</u> while Europe was busy fighting World War I.
3) The USA was <u>worried</u> about Japanese <u>competition</u>, and tried to <u>limit</u> its power and <u>reduce</u> the size of its navy.
4) When the Depression <u>wrecked</u> Japanese industries, the military leaders and business interests in Japan called for <u>military expansion</u> to strengthen the country.

Japanese Aggression led to the Manchurian Crisis

1) Japan had a <u>large</u> army and navy. Since 1905, it had <u>controlled</u> Korea and the territory of the South Manchurian Railway.
2) In September 1931, it used the excuse of a disturbance to <u>take</u> Mukden and send its troops to <u>overrun</u> the rest of Manchuria.
3) The Japanese <u>pretended</u> to give Manchuria independence. They put a weak leader called <u>Puyi</u> (who'd been the last emperor of China) on the throne so they could <u>control him</u>.
4) The League of Nations sent Lord Lytton to <u>assess</u> the situation. He produced a <u>report</u>, which said the Japanese had been <u>wrong</u>, but the League <u>didn't do</u> anything else — it failed to stop Japan and end the crisis.

> This was the <u>first major challenge</u> for the League of Nations, and the whole world saw it <u>fail</u> to confront the Japanese aggression.

The League was Weakened

1) Japan <u>refused</u> to accept Lord Lytton's report and <u>withdrew</u> from the League in 1933.
2) In 1933 the Japanese <u>invaded</u> China's Jehol Province, which bordered Manchuria.
3) Dictators like Hitler and Mussolini saw the obvious <u>weakness</u> of the League.
4) Japan signed a <u>treaty</u> with Germany in 1936, and in 1937 started to <u>invade</u> China — again the League did <u>nothing</u> to stop it.

The League of Nations — a Drama out of a Crisis...

This is where things started to go <u>seriously wrong</u> for the League of Nations. Japan's suffering in the Depression made it look for ways to get stronger — by <u>expanding</u> and <u>attacking</u> other countries. The League's weakness meant it'd be a matter of time before <u>someone else</u> tried too.

The Invasion of Abyssinia

Next it was the Italians who tested the strength of the League of Nations.

Italy was ruled by Mussolini's Fascists

1) Italy was under the control of Benito Mussolini and his Fascist Party.
2) Mussolini had been made Prime Minister in 1922 after threatening to take power by marching on Rome. He used his new position to change the voting rules, and in the 1924 election the Fascists swept to power.
3) From 1925, he began to change Italy into a dictatorship.
4) Opposition political parties were banned. He used a harsh secret police against his opponents.

In the early 1930s, Mussolini was more on the side of France and Britain. He joined them at the Stresa Conference in 1935 to stand against a possible German invasion of Austria.

Mussolini Invaded Abyssinia for Four Reasons

1) Italy had been defeated by Abyssinia in 1896 and the Italians wanted revenge.
2) Abyssinia — now called Ethiopia — was well positioned for Italy to add to her lands in Africa.
3) Mussolini had seen Japan get away with the Manchurian invasion despite the League of Nations' threats.
4) Mussolini dreamed of making Italy a great empire again.

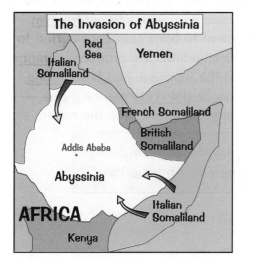

The Invasion of Abyssinia
Red Sea
Yemen
Italian Somaliland
French Somaliland
British Somaliland
Addis Ababa
Abyssinia
AFRICA
Italian Somaliland
Kenya

1) In October 1935, Mussolini sent troops with heavy artillery and tanks to invade.
2) The Abyssinian leader appealed directly to the League of Nations for help.
3) The League of Nations imposed economic sanctions, but delayed banning oil exports in case the USA didn't support them.
4) Britain and France didn't close the Suez Canal to Italian ships — so supplies got through despite the sanctions.
5) By May 1936 Italy had conquered all of Abyssinia.

The League of Nations appeared Ineffective

1) The League's reputation was in tatters. But Italy became more confident — and started making pacts with the fascist leader of Germany, Adolf Hitler.
2) Mussolini and Hitler agreed the Rome-Berlin Axis in 1936, and in 1937 Italy joined Japan and Germany in the Anti-Comintern Pact.
3) Italy also attacked Albania in 1938, and signed the Pact of Steel with Hitler in 1939.

Some world problems were out of its league...

Once again, the League was too weak and ineffective. Its failure to protect Abyssinia would have dire consequences. The new alliance between Mussolini's Italy and Hitler's Germany gave Germany the extra strength it needed to bounce back after the losses of Versailles.

The Failure of the League of Nations

It's important to see <u>why</u> the idea of the League of Nations <u>didn't work</u>.

The League <u>Didn't Achieve</u> its original Aims

The League set out to prevent <u>aggression</u>, to encourage <u>cooperation</u>, to work towards <u>disarmament</u> and to prevent a major <u>war</u> breaking out again. In the end, it failed on all these.

The League did have some <u>success</u> in improving the lives of ordinary people around the world — combating slavery and poor working conditions — but this <u>wasn't</u> its main purpose.

There are <u>Arguments in Defence of the League...</u>

It was always going to be tough...
1) Once the USA <u>refused to join</u>, Britain and France had a very difficult task — when they <u>weren't</u> that <u>strong</u> themselves. You can't enforce sanctions if nobody else wants to do it.
2) The <u>Depression</u> made the political situation <u>tougher</u> worldwide — it was nobody's fault.
3) <u>No organisation</u> could have <u>stopped</u> leaders like Mussolini or Hitler peacefully. Italy and Germany were members themselves, and could have worked harder for the League instead of against it. The same was true of Japan.
4) The League of Nations had to <u>defend</u> a settlement made after World War I which many of the nations themselves thought was <u>unfair</u>.

...and there are <u>Arguments Against</u> the League

It made some big mistakes...
1) The <u>Manchurian</u> crisis was the turning point — the League should have <u>resisted</u> Japan.
2) Too many members <u>didn't</u> keep to the <u>rules</u>. When they were attacked for it, they simply <u>left</u> the League, e.g. Germany and Japan in 1933, Italy in 1937.
3) Britain and France <u>didn't lead strongly</u>, and were often very <u>slow</u> to do things.
4) Members of the League who could have <u>opposed</u> aggression <u>didn't</u> want to <u>risk</u> a war.
5) <u>Ambitious</u> members like Hitler and Mussolini <u>weren't dealt</u> with strongly enough.
6) Instead of cooperation, it let the old system of secret <u>alliances</u> creep back.

For	Against
• Early successes in preserving peace between minor powers	• Rise of dictators
	• Manchurian crisis 1931
	• Failed to force countries to disarm
• Helped to rebuild Europe and aid refugees of the war	• Germany and Japan leave 1933
	• Abyssinian crisis 1935
• Improved health and labour conditions around the world	• Rome-Berlin Axis 1936
	• German aggression
• Kellogg-Briand Pact 1928	• Italy leaves 1937
	• USSR expelled from League 1939
• Provided the groundwork for the United Nations	• Powerless to prevent World War II

For and against — now you be the judge...

Make sure you know the League's <u>original aims</u> and can give your own verdict on whether the League can be <u>blamed</u> for its problems, or if they were <u>unavoidable</u>.

The Rise of the Dictators

Poor conditions in 1930s Europe saw the rise of <u>dictators</u>, and increasing international <u>tension</u>.

Problems and Fears aided the rise of Dictators

Dictatorship might seem a scary idea, but for some people it solved a lot of <u>worrying issues</u>.

1) **THE LOCARNO TREATY** in 1925 had settled the <u>western</u> borders of Germany. But the borders on the East were vulnerable if Germany wanted to expand — people wanted strong leaders to <u>protect</u> them.

2) **DEPRESSION** still affected most countries, causing widespread <u>unemployment</u> and <u>poverty</u>. People welcomed <u>strong governments</u> who promised to put things right.

3) **DEMOCRACY** was often <u>blamed</u> for the bad conditions — democratic governments seemed unable to prevent them happening or to improve the situation.

4) **COMMUNISM** was seen as a threat to all of Europe after the Russian Revolution in 1917 — people looked to strong leaders to fight the threat of <u>world revolution</u> by the workers.

5) **ISOLATIONISM** continued — the USA <u>stayed out</u> of world affairs, and Britain and France weren't strong enough to oppose the large numbers of foreign dictators.

6) **FRANCE** was still suspicious of Germany and was building <u>strong defences</u> along the Maginot Line — many Germans felt they needed a strong leader against this French threat.

7) **DISARMAMENT FAILED** — most countries <u>refused to disarm</u> to the same level as Germany in 1932. Germany saw this as <u>unfair</u> and became determined to rebuild its armed forces.

Dictatorships popped up All Over Europe

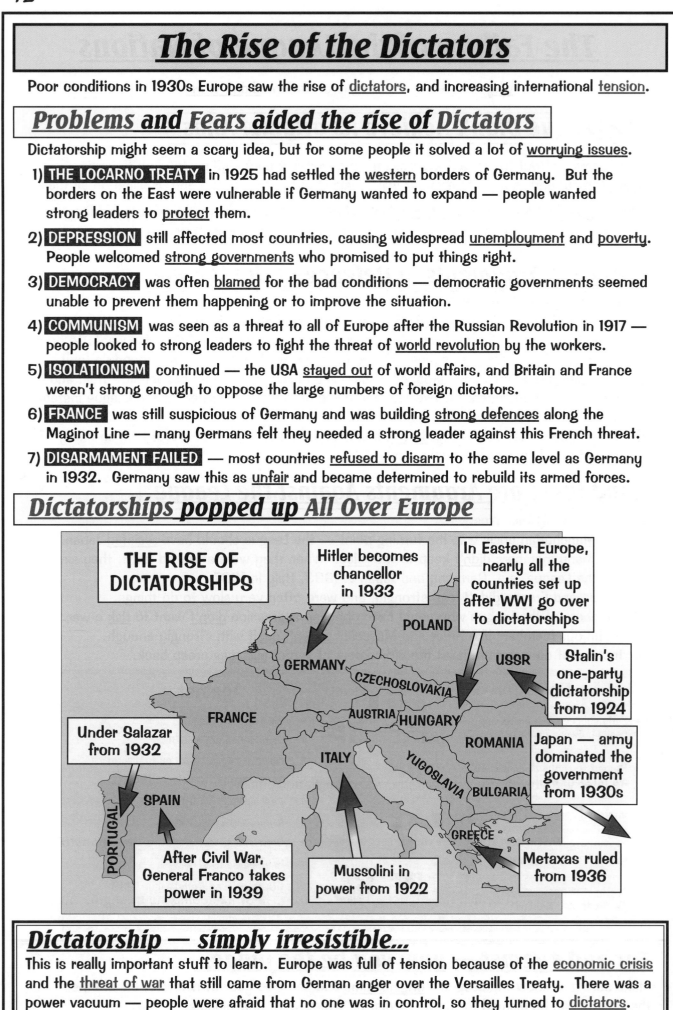

THE RISE OF DICTATORSHIPS

Hitler becomes chancellor in 1933

In Eastern Europe, nearly all the countries set up after WWI go over to dictatorships

POLAND

GERMANY

CZECHOSLOVAKIA

USSR

Stalin's one-party dictatorship from 1924

FRANCE

AUSTRIA HUNGARY

Under Salazar from 1932

ROMANIA

Japan — army dominated the government from 1930s

ITALY

YUGOSLAVIA

BULGARIA

PORTUGAL

SPAIN

GREECE

Metaxas ruled from 1936

After Civil War, General Franco takes power in 1939

Mussolini in power from 1922

Dictatorship — simply irresistible...

This is really important stuff to learn. Europe was full of tension because of the <u>economic crisis</u> and the <u>threat of war</u> that still came from German anger over the Versailles Treaty. There was a power vacuum — people were afraid that no one was in control, so they turned to <u>dictators</u>.

Hitler's Foreign Policy

Hitler rose to power during a time of depression and international tensions in Europe — and his aggressive foreign policy just made things worse...

The atmosphere in Europe was Tense

1) All the League of Nations' attempts at disarmament had failed.
2) Democracy had collapsed in much of Europe. Several countries were led by aggressive leaders who wanted to take over new territories, and weren't worried about defying the League of Nations.
3) Japan and Italy both invaded other countries' territory (see p.9-10) — and the League of Nations did virtually nothing to stop them.
4) Germany still resented its treatment after the First World War.
5) France had never stopped distrusting Germany.
6) Britain didn't want to get dragged into a war, whatever the reason.

German discontent helped Hitler rise to Power

1) During the Depression, extremist parties flourished (see p.8). There was widespread poverty and unemployment — people wanted strong leadership.
2) Adolf Hitler, the leader of the Nazi Party, came to power in Germany in 1933.
3) The main aims of Hitler's foreign policy were:

1) He wanted the Versailles Treaty to be overturned. Hitler hated the treaty which he saw as unfairly weakening Germany (see p.4).
2) He wanted rearmament. Germany had been forced to reduce its armed forces under the Versailles Treaty. Hitler wanted Germany to be a strong military power.
3) He wanted all German-speaking peoples to be united in a German Reich (empire). This would mean annexing Austria, and taking territory from Poland and Czechoslovakia which had German minorities. This idea was known as Grossdeutschland — meaning "Great Germany".
4) He wanted to expand Germany's territory by taking land from peoples he saw as inferior, such as the Slavs in the east of Europe. This expansion would provide more Lebensraum (which means "living space") for the German people.

Hitler Prepared for German Expansion

1) In 1933, Hitler withdrew Germany from the League of Nations' Disarmament Conference. He later withdrew Germany from the League of Nations itself.
2) In 1934, Hitler agreed a 10-year friendship pact with Poland — which had the effect of weakening Poland's alliance with France.
3) In March 1935, he brought in military conscription in Germany — breaking the terms of the Versailles Treaty. This was condemned by France, Britain and Italy.
4) In June 1935, Hitler reached a naval agreement with Britain. It allowed Germany to build up to 35% of British naval strength and up to 45% of its submarine strength. This agreement implied that Germany had a right to rearm — breaking the Treaty of Versailles.

Hitler didn't lack ambition...

Hitler was an ambitious and ruthless leader. He wanted to make Germany a strong military power which could dominate Europe — and didn't care if he broke the rules to do it.

The Rhineland and Austria

Hitler's foreign policy became increasingly <u>aggressive</u>...

Hitler's first Territorial Success was in the Saar

1) The Saar was an <u>industrialised</u> region of Germany about 30 miles wide, <u>bordering France</u>.
2) Under the Treaty of Versailles, the Saar was put under the <u>control</u> of the <u>League of Nations</u> for 15 years from 1920. The plan was for the territory's status to be decided by <u>popular vote</u> in 1935.
3) In the January 1935 <u>plebiscite</u> (referendum), 90% of voters chose <u>reunion</u> with <u>Germany</u> — showing Hitler's popularity. The Saar was <u>returned</u> to <u>Germany</u> in March.

In March 1936 Hitler sent Troops into the Rhineland

1) The Rhineland was <u>demilitarised</u> by the <u>Treaty of Versailles</u>. Germany accepted this by signing the <u>Locarno Treaties</u> in 1925 (see p.36).
2) But the <u>League of Nations</u> was busy with Italy's <u>invasion of Abyssinia</u>. Hitler saw his chance.
3) Russia and France had recently made a <u>treaty</u> against German attacks. Hitler claimed that this <u>threatened Germany</u>, and that he should be allowed to put troops on Germany's borders.
4) Hitler reckoned Britain wouldn't get involved. But he was <u>unsure</u> how France would react.
5) The German forces had orders to <u>pull out immediately</u> if the French army moved in. But France was in the middle of an <u>election campaign</u> — so no one was willing to <u>start a war</u> with Germany. The League of Nations and Britain were angry but <u>refused to take action</u>.

> Hitler was <u>breaking</u> part of the Treaty of Versailles — and no one tried to <u>stop</u> him.

Hitler then turned his attention to Austria

1) Hitler believed Germany and Austria belonged <u>together</u>. He wanted "<u>Anschluss</u>" (union).
2) In 1934, a <u>Nazi revolt</u> in Austria <u>failed</u>, after Mussolini moved Italian troops to the Austrian border, scaring Hitler off.
3) But by <u>1936</u>, Hitler and Mussolini had become <u>allies</u>.
4) Hitler encouraged Austrian Nazis to stage <u>demonstrations</u> and <u>protests</u>. In February 1938, he demanded that an Austrian Nazi called <u>Seyss-Inquart</u> be made <u>Minister of the Interior</u>.
5) Instead, the Austrian Chancellor Schuschnigg called a <u>plebiscite</u> on whether Austria should remain independent. But Hitler <u>couldn't be sure</u> he'd get the result he wanted.
6) Hitler threatened to <u>invade</u> if Schuschnigg didn't resign. Schuschnigg couldn't take the risk — he and his cabinet <u>resigned</u>, except for Seyss-Inquart, who <u>invited</u> the German army into Austria to "restore order".

> On 15th March 1938, Hitler entered Vienna to proclaim the <u>Greater German Reich</u>. Austria and Germany were <u>united</u>.

The late 1930s — storm clouds gathering...

Hitler was rapidly <u>gaining power</u> — after the humiliations of Versailles, Germany was on the up. Write a list of the <u>main reasons</u> why Hitler <u>got away with</u> sending troops into the Rhineland.

Czechoslovakia and Munich 1938

Czechoslovakia was afraid that Hitler, after taking over Austria, would try the same thing on them.

Hitler put Pressure on Czechoslovakia in 1938

1) Czechoslovakia's borders had been set at Versailles. The Sudetenland was a part of western Czechoslovakia which had a large population of Germans — about 3 million.
2) Britain, France and the USSR agreed to support the Czechs if Hitler invaded.
3) Hitler promised the British PM, Neville Chamberlain, that he wouldn't invade Czechoslovakia.
4) But soon Hitler claimed that the Czech government was discriminating against the Germans in the Sudetenland. The Nazis organised demonstrations in the Sudetenland demanding that the area should become part of Germany.
5) In May 1938, Hitler threatened to go to war. The Czech leader, Benes, was ready to fight.
6) But Chamberlain and the French PM Daladier then put pressure on the Czechs to give concessions to Hitler to avoid a war.

Chamberlain Negotiated with Hitler

1) In September 1938, Chamberlain flew twice to Germany, where he met Hitler to negotiate.
2) But Hitler changed his demands, and set a date of 1st October to "rescue" the Sudeten Germans. Chamberlain called this unreasonable, and the British Navy was mobilised for war.
3) Then on 29th September, Hitler invited Chamberlain, Daladier and Mussolini to a conference in Munich. Mussolini put forward a plan (really written by the German Foreign Office).
4) After discussions, the four leaders produced the Munich Agreement. This gave the Sudetenland to Germany but guaranteed the rest of Czechoslovakia would stay put. Chamberlain gave in to Hitler's demands because he believed Hitler would honour his promise.

The Munich Agreement was all about appeasement — giving aggressive countries like Germany and Italy what they wanted in order to avoid a major war.

Not Everyone was Happy with the Munich Agreement

1) It seemed like Chamberlain had prevented war. He claimed the agreement meant "peace for our time", and he flew back to Britain to a hero's welcome.
2) But Czechoslovakia and the USSR weren't invited to the Munich Conference. So the Czechs weren't even consulted on their own future.
3) And the USSR, who had big concerns about Hitler, were horrified at the agreement.

Appeasement may seem a bad idea now, but at the time, many people supported it.
1) No one in Britain wanted a war, and some people felt the Treaty of Versailles was unfair to Germany — so Hitler should be allowed to rebuild its power.
2) Many British politicians feared communism and the USSR much more than Hitler — they wanted Germany as a buffer between Britain and the USSR.
3) Britain's economy and armed forces were weak. Some historians say Chamberlain gave in to Hitler in order to buy time for rearming.

Appeasement — "Peace for our Time"...

Make sure you know what appeasement was — and scribble a list of the events of the Czech crisis.

Poland and the Outbreak of War

Most people were <u>glad</u> there wouldn't be a war — but in a poll soon after the Munich Agreement, over 90% of British people asked said they <u>didn't trust</u> Hitler.

In March 1939 Hitler took over the Rest of Czechoslovakia

1) After losing the Sudetenland, Czechoslovakia began to descend into <u>anarchy</u>. Slovakia began to demand <u>independence</u>.
2) Hitler persuaded the Czech president to <u>allow German troops in</u> to "restore order".
3) In May 1939, Germany signed the "<u>Pact of Steel</u>" with Italy. They promised to support each other if war was declared.
4) Britain and France <u>did nothing</u> — but it was clear that the appeasement policy had <u>failed</u>. Hitler had <u>broken his promises</u> and taken non-German lands.
5) Once the Nazis had taken the rest of Czechoslovakia, Britain <u>abandoned</u> appeasement and made an <u>agreement</u> with <u>Poland</u> to support it in case it was invaded.

The USSR made a Pact with Hitler

1) The USSR (Soviet Union) <u>joined</u> the League of Nations in 1934, and signed a <u>treaty</u> with France in 1935 <u>against</u> Hitler. The Soviet leader, Stalin, was <u>suspicious</u> of the Nazis.
2) But the USSR <u>never trusted</u> the French, and <u>couldn't</u> understand why nobody stood up to Hitler earlier. After Munich, Stalin decided to <u>negotiate</u> with Germany to <u>protect</u> the USSR.

3) The <u>Nazi-Soviet Pact</u> was signed in August 1939. The USSR and Germany agreed <u>not</u> to attack each other. They also <u>secretly planned</u> to carve up another country — <u>Poland</u>.
4) They agreed that if Germany invaded Poland, the USSR would get Latvia, Estonia, Finland and East Poland — but Hitler <u>never</u> really <u>intended</u> to let them keep those areas.

On <u>1st September 1939</u> Hitler <u>invaded Poland</u>. This was too much — Britain and France ordered him to leave. He ignored them and Britain <u>declared war</u> on Germany on <u>3rd September 1939</u>.

The Road to the Second World War

These are the <u>three key areas</u> you need to cover in your revision of this topic:
1) Make sure you learn the final steps to war between 1936 and 1939 — the <u>sequence of events</u> is very important and you should practise the different names and spellings.
2) Be clear on the <u>reasons</u> why nobody stopped Hitler sooner — e.g. the <u>weakness</u> of the League of Nations, the policy of <u>appeasement</u> and the <u>secret plotting</u> of the USSR etc.
3) Remember the <u>long-term causes</u> of tension during the 1920s and 1930s — think about the <u>problems</u> caused by the Versailles Treaty and the League of Nations, and the <u>consequences</u> of the worldwide economic problems during the Depression.

Twenty years on — Europe was at war again...

This is really important stuff. Remember — there were <u>long-term causes</u> as well as the <u>short-term ones</u>. Scribble a quick summary of the <u>Nazi-Soviet pact</u>. Then test your memory of Hitler's actions in the Rhineland, Austria, Sudetenland, Czechoslovakia and Poland.

Revision Summary

Time for some magnificent mind-bending questions — just so you know how you're getting on. The important thing is to see what you know, and to work out what you don't. Then go back over the section and have another go at these spiffing questions. Keep at it until you can get every single one of them right — I know it sounds much too hard, but you can do it... It's the only way to win yourself top marks when the exams come around.

1) Who were the 'big three' who led the talks at Versailles?

2) Who came up with the Fourteen Points?

3) Which area of Germany was demilitarised?

4) What was Article 231 of the Versailles Treaty?

5) How much was Germany expected to pay in damages? What were the payments called?

6) What were 'mandates'?

7) Give three reasons why the Treaty of Versailles could be seen as fair.

8) Give three reasons why the Treaty of Versailles could be seen as too harsh.

9) Explain why the Germans hated the Treaty of Versailles.

10) Name the other treaties which followed Versailles. Write briefly what each one did.

11) List the four main aims of the League of Nations.

12) Which countries were permanent members of the Council?

13) Name three early successes which the League enjoyed.

14) Give four reasons why the USA would not accept membership of the League of Nations.

15) Why did Britain and France find it difficult to lead the League?

16) Which two important nations apart from the USA were not members at the beginning?

17) What event sparked off the global depression in 1929?

18) The Depression started in America. How did it affect other countries?

19) Why did the USA see Japan as a threat?

20) Why did Japan invade Manchuria?

21) Why did the Manchurian crisis make the League of Nations look weak?

22) Give four reasons why Italy invaded Abyssinia in 1935.

23) Who signed the Pact of Steel?

24) Give four ways in which the League of Nations' task was made very difficult.

25) Give four ways in which the League of Nations could be judged a failure.

26) List as many reasons as you can why several dictators came to power in Europe in the 1930s.

27) Give four aims of Adolf Hitler's foreign policy in the 1930s.

28) When did Hitler bring in military conscription in Germany?

29) Where did Germany send troops in 1936? Explain why nobody stopped them.

30) What was the name given to the joining of Germany and Austria? How did Hitler achieve it?

31) Name the area of Czechoslovakia that Hitler wanted in 1938.

32) What was agreed in the Munich Agreement in 1938?

33) What was appeasement? Give three reasons why it was a popular policy in Britain at the time.

34) Why did the Soviet Union make an agreement with Germany in 1939?

35) Explain four causes of the Second World War.

The Second World War 1939-1945

The Second World War was the <u>biggest</u>, most <u>destructive</u> war in history. It lasted from 1939-1945.

Warfare Had Moved On Since The First World War

1) This time the fighting really was <u>worldwide</u> — from the desert to the Arctic, from mountains to jungle, on land, sea and in the air. Fighting raged through Europe, Africa, Asia, and the Pacific.

2) <u>Technology</u> had <u>advanced</u> in 20 years — aircraft and tanks had been of limited use in the First War. This would be a war of <u>rapid movement</u> — without trench war stalemate.

3) <u>Civilian populations</u> were even more <u>affected</u> — by advances in bombing technology, evacuation, occupation, and shortages etc. Many people still remembered the First War — no-one celebrated this time. The <u>economy</u> and <u>society</u> of each country at war were soon geared to helping the <u>war effort</u>.

The Chronology Of The Second World War

| War in Europe | War in N Africa | War in Asia/Pacific |

Axis victories

Allied victories

1939
September: Germany invades Poland. Britain declares war.

1940
April/May: Germany invades Norway, Holland, and France. Evacuation of British troops (Dunkirk).

June: France defeated. Italy declares war on Britain and France.
August: Battle of Britain. War in the air.

1941
June: Germany attacks USSR (Russia) (Operation Barbarossa).

December: Japanese attack Pearl Harbor. USA declares war. Japan invades SE Asia.

1942
June: Pacific victory for USA at Battle of Midway.

July/October: victory for Allies at El Alamein. North Africa desert war.

1943
February: Russian counter-attack and victory at Stalingrad.

September: Italy surrenders to the Allies.

1944
June: Allies land in Normandy, northern France (D-Day).

1945
February: Allies invade Germany.
May: Germany surrenders to Soviet army.

May: Major allied air attacks begin on Japan.
August: Atomic bombs dropped on Hiroshima and Nagasaki. Japan surrenders.

The Second World War — a war of speed and movement...

You don't need to learn the chronology of the war — but making sure you're familiar with what happened is great background for the rest of this section.

Planning the Post-War Future

The <u>main winners</u> of World War II were Britain, the USSR and the USA. Two main <u>summits</u> were held between the Big Three allies during 1945 to decide on the future of Germany and Eastern Europe. These were the <u>Yalta</u> conference and the <u>Potsdam</u> conference.

There were Three Major Decisions at Yalta in 1945

The "big three" allied leaders — British Prime Minister <u>Winston Churchill</u>, US President <u>Roosevelt</u> and USSR leader <u>Stalin</u> — met for the <u>Yalta Conference</u> in February 1945 — to plan what they wanted to happen <u>after</u> the war (although the conflict was still ongoing at this point).

1) Germany was to be <u>split</u> into four zones of occupation.
2) <u>Free elections</u> for new governments would be held in countries previously occupied in Eastern Europe.
3) The <u>United Nations</u> would <u>replace</u> the failed League of Nations.

Then the Situation Changed

1) Roosevelt died and was succeeded by <u>Harry Truman</u>, who was <u>suspicious</u> of the USSR.
2) In Britain, the Conservative PM Winston Churchill was replaced by Labour's <u>Clement Attlee</u>.
3) The USSR <u>expanded westwards</u> into the Baltic states and parts of Finland, Poland, Czechoslovakia and Romania.

The allies were now <u>suspicious</u> of each other. Stalin wanted to <u>control Eastern Europe</u> so didn't want elections there — the USA and Britain suspected this. Truman and Attlee were new to their jobs — Stalin thought they'd be <u>weak leaders</u> so he could do <u>whatever he wanted</u>.

Agreements were Made at Potsdam in August 1945

<u>Germany surrendered</u> in <u>May 1945</u>. The allies made more decisions about <u>post-war Europe</u>:
1) The new <u>boundaries</u> of <u>Poland</u> were agreed.
2) The allies decided to <u>divide</u> Germany and Berlin between them.
3) They agreed to legal <u>trials</u> at Nuremberg of Nazi leaders for <u>war crimes</u>.

The USA and USSR had very Different Ideologies

Although the USA and USSR had been <u>allies</u> during the Second World War they had very different beliefs. The USSR was <u>communist</u>. The USA was <u>capitalist</u>. After the end of the Second World War, the two countries became <u>rivals</u>.

1) Economically, communism meant <u>state control</u> of industry and agriculture. The USA, by contrast, valued <u>private enterprise</u> — the 'American Dream' was that anyone could work their way to the top to be <u>wealthy and successful</u>.
2) Politically, communism meant a <u>one-party state</u>. The USA valued <u>political freedom</u>.
3) Communism aimed at world <u>revolution</u>, and so it was seen by Americans as a <u>danger</u> to their <u>democracy</u>. Likewise, the communists feared worldwide <u>American influence</u>.

Yalta learn this page — it's important...

Plenty for you to learn here — things changed fast after the war. Remember two of the Big Three <u>changed leaders</u> — you need to know what <u>difference</u> this made.

Increasing Tensions

After World War Two, the USA and USSR were the major world superpowers.
Unfortunately, relations between them went rapidly downhill...

The USA and the USSR began an Arms Race

The USA and USSR became very competitive — each wanting to be the strongest, and feeling
threatened by the other. There was an arms race to have the most powerful weapons.

1) Germany surrendered in May 1945, but the war against Japan continued. In August 1945,
the USA dropped two atom bombs on Japan — destroying the cities of Hiroshima and
Nagasaki. These bombs were incredibly powerful and thousands of civilians were killed.
Japan surrendered immediately after this.

2) The USA had kept the atom bomb (A-bomb) secret from the USSR until just before it was
used in Japan. For four years, the USA was the world's only nuclear power.

3) But in 1949, the USSR exploded their own A-bomb. The USA developed the even more
powerful hydrogen bomb (H-bomb) in 1952. The USSR had followed with their own by 1955.

The USSR became Influential in Eastern Europe

1) At the end of the Second World War, the USSR's Red Army occupied Eastern Europe. Stalin
had no intention of keeping the promise he made at Yalta to allow free elections in Poland.

2) Between 1945 and 1948, Stalin installed pro-Soviet "puppet" governments in Poland,
Hungary, Romania, Bulgaria and Czechoslovakia. Free speech was suppressed.

3) Non-communist parties were banned, and even communist parties were controlled by the
Cominform (Communist Information Bureau) to consist solely of Russian-style communists.

4) Comecon (the Council for Mutual Economic Assistance), set up in 1949, worked to
nationalise the states' industries and collectivise agriculture.

5) For a while it seemed that Czechoslovakia might remain democratic. But when the Communist
Party seemed likely to lose ground in the next election, it seized power in February 1948.

6) The exception to Soviet domination was Yugoslavia, which had freed itself from the Germans
without the Red Army. Yugoslavia was communist but more open to the West. Its leader,
Tito, argued with Stalin over political interference. Stalin cut off aid but didn't invade.

There was an 'Iron Curtain' between East and West

1) Increasing tensions between the USA and the USSR
became known as the 'Cold War'.

2) It was called the Cold War because there wasn't any
direct fighting — instead both sides tried to gain the
upper hand with alliances and plans.

3) Both sides were afraid of another war because of the
huge power of atomic weapons.

4) Countries in Western Europe tended to support the
USA. Most countries in Eastern Europe were
dominated by the USSR.

5) In a famous speech, Winston Churchill warned there
was an Iron Curtain dividing Europe.

The Iron Curtain — it just wouldn't wash...

Nuclear weapons were capable of wiping out entire cities in one go — people thought it could
be the end of humankind if a proper war broke out, which is why both sides were so cautious.

US Influence and the Berlin Blockade

If there was one thing the USA <u>didn't want</u>, it was for the whole world to go <u>communist</u>.

The USA was Worried about the Spread of Communism

<u>President Truman</u> was worried that other countries might also fall to communism. Truman tried to <u>stop the spread</u> of communism in two main ways:

1) The Marshall Plan

This promised American <u>aid</u> to European countries to help <u>rebuild</u> their <u>economies</u> — West Germany benefited massively. The USA was worried that if Western Europe remained <u>weak</u> it might be vulnerable to <u>communism</u>.

2) The Truman Doctrine

The USA would <u>support</u> any nation threatened by a communist <u>takeover</u>. For example, the USA gave <u>$400 million</u> of aid to <u>Turkey</u> and <u>Greece</u> to try to stop communism spreading. A <u>civil war</u> had started in Greece in 1946 between the <u>pro-Western government</u> and <u>communists</u> — Truman wanted to give the government all the help he could.

In 1948 the USSR and the West Disagreed over Berlin

1) There were <u>four zones</u> of occupied Berlin. The USA and Britain agreed to <u>combine</u> their zones into a zone called <u>Bizonia</u> in 1947.
2) The French agreed to combine their zone with them — the new western zone had a <u>single government</u>, and a <u>new</u> currency to help economic recovery.
3) The Soviet Union <u>opposed</u> these moves. Stalin wanted to keep Germany weak — so he decided to <u>blockade</u> Berlin.
4) Berlin was in Eastern Germany, which was controlled by the USSR — so Stalin ordered that all <u>land communication</u> between West Berlin and the outside world should be <u>cut off</u>.

West Berlin survived because of the <u>Berlin Airlift</u>. Between June 1948 and May 1949, the only way of <u>obtaining supplies</u> from the outside world was <u>by air</u>. By 1949, 8000 tons of supplies were being flown into West Berlin each day.

In 1949 Stalin Ended the Blockade

1) <u>Two new states</u> were formed — West Germany (German Federal Republic) and communist East Germany (German Democratic Republic).
2) In 1949 the Western Powers formed <u>NATO</u> (the North Atlantic Treaty Organisation) against the communist threat. The Eastern Bloc formed the <u>Warsaw Pact</u> in 1955 — a military treaty designed to counter NATO.

Two Germanies — and two German football teams...

Don't forget, the Cold War <u>never</u> led to any real fighting between the USA and USSR. Instead they seemed to be playing a giant game of chess. Make sure you know the <u>two US policies</u> intended to stop Europe turning communist, and the events that led to Germany being split up.

The Cuban Missile Crisis

Stalin died in 1953 and his successor, <u>Khrushchev</u>, seemed more <u>friendly</u> towards the USA — he visited in 1959. However, the USA was keen to keep all <u>countries close to its shores</u> friendly, too.

Cuba *is Only 100 Miles from the USA*

Fidel Castro

1) Since 1952, Cuba had been <u>ruled</u> by Batista, a ruthless and corrupt military <u>dictator</u>. Batista allowed American businessmen and the Mafia to make <u>huge profits</u> in a country where <u>most people</u> lived in <u>poverty</u>.
2) In 1953 <u>Fidel Castro</u> attempted to <u>overthrow</u> the government, but he was <u>defeated</u> and <u>imprisoned</u>. After his release in 1955, he fled Cuba.
3) In 1956 Castro returned and began a <u>guerrilla war</u>. By 1959, he had enough support to take Cuba's capital, Havana, and <u>successfully</u> overthrow the government.

Castro *wanted to Get Rid of American Influence*

1) Castro made a big impact. He <u>shut down</u> the gambling casinos and the brothels. He also <u>nationalised</u> American-owned sugar mills.
2) The USA <u>cut off</u> diplomatic <u>relations</u> with Cuba.
3) Castro began to work with the USSR — he'd always been <u>influenced</u> by <u>communism</u>.
4) The USSR offered to buy Cuba's sugar <u>instead</u> of the USA.

Cuban Rebels *in America plotted an Invasion*

1) In 1961, President Kennedy authorised a CIA-trained <u>invasion</u> of Cuba by anti-Castro rebels.
2) In April 1961, the rebels landed in the <u>Bay of Pigs</u>, but the USA <u>didn't give</u> them <u>air support</u> as they had promised. The rebels were easily <u>defeated</u> — it was a bit of a fiasco.
3) This invasion meant Castro decided that Cuba needed <u>Soviet military assistance</u>.

Soviet Nuclear Missiles *were shipped to Cuba*

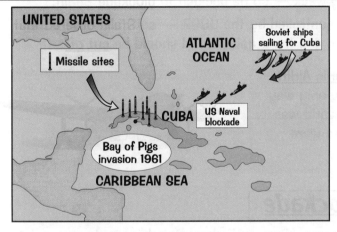

1) In 1962, the USA's U-2 spy planes <u>detected</u> Soviet missiles in Cuba. From Cuba these missiles could be used to <u>attack</u> US cities with very little warning.
2) President Kennedy ordered a <u>naval blockade</u> of Cuba. All Soviet ships were to be <u>stopped</u> and <u>searched</u> to prevent further missiles being transported to Cuba.
3) Kennedy <u>demanded</u> that Khrushchev <u>withdraw</u> his missiles, and <u>prepared to invade</u> Cuba. The Soviet ships steamed on to Cuba.
4) The world was on the brink of <u>nuclear war</u>...

In the end, Khrushchev made a deal to <u>remove</u> the missiles from Cuba and ordered his <u>ships</u> to <u>turn around</u>. In exchange the US <u>lifted</u> the <u>blockade</u>, promised to <u>not invade</u> Cuba — and <u>secretly</u> agreed to <u>remove</u> their <u>missiles</u> from <u>Turkey</u>, which borders the USSR.

U-2 were spy planes — I always thought they were a rock band...

The <u>13 days</u> of the Cuban missile crisis were the closest the world's been to nuclear war. There was a <u>stalemate</u> — if one side fired, so would the other and <u>everyone</u> would be destroyed. Future clashes had to be avoided — in 1963 a telephone <u>hotline</u> was set up between the Kremlin and the White House.

Vietnam and the USA

In 1954, <u>Vietnam</u> became independent of France. It was split into two parts — the <u>communist North</u> and the <u>democratic South</u>.

The USA got involved to *Stop Communism Spreading*

The Domino Theory

The <u>domino theory</u> says that when you knock over the first domino in a line the rest will fall down too. The USA thought that the same was true of communism — if <u>one country</u> became <u>communist</u> soon all the <u>nearby countries</u> would do the same. So China, North Korea and North Vietnam could all turn South Vietnam communist.

President Eisenhower, and later Kennedy, gave democratic <u>South Vietnam</u> lots of <u>assistance</u> — such as <u>financial aid</u> and <u>military 'advisors'</u>. This was part of the Truman Doctrine (p.21).

In 1963 *President Johnson* changed *US Policy*

The President was <u>determined</u> to keep South Vietnam <u>free</u> from <u>communism</u>:
1) He <u>increased troop numbers</u> from 23 000 in 1964 to 180 000 in 1965 and 500 000 in 1967.
2) He began a <u>bombing campaign</u> against communist North Vietnam.

The war became *Unpopular in the USA*

1) The <u>Tet Offensive</u> by the North Vietnamese in 1968 took the Americans by <u>surprise</u>.
2) The offensive was beaten but there were <u>heavy casualties</u> — about 14 000 US soldiers were killed in action in 1968.
3) The American public saw <u>brutal images</u> of the war on <u>TV</u>. They were also shocked by news of the 1968 <u>My Lai massacre</u> where civilians were murdered by US troops.
4) The war was very <u>expensive</u> — it cost millions of dollars.

President *Nixon tried to Finish the war*

1) American troops were gradually <u>withdrawn</u> from Vietnam — in 1972 only 47 000 were left.
2) Instead the US started <u>training</u> the South Vietnamese to fight the <u>Vietcong</u> — the communist guerrillas fighting in South Vietnam.
3) Heavy <u>bombing</u> of North Vietnam and Cambodia began, which aimed to <u>destroy</u> North Vietnamese <u>supply lines</u> — the Ho Chi Minh trail. It was hoped this would <u>force</u> a <u>peace</u> settlement.
4) In 1973 a <u>ceasefire</u> was agreed and the US <u>pulled out</u> — but fighting <u>continued</u> between the North and South. In 1975 the South Vietnamese capital <u>Saigon</u> was <u>captured</u> by the North.

There were *6 main Reasons why the USA was Defeated*

1) The Vietcong treated the South Vietnamese <u>well</u> and gained their <u>support</u>.
2) American bombing killed many <u>civilians</u> and made North Vietnam more <u>determined</u>.
3) Vietcong guerrillas were very <u>skilful</u> soldiers. They didn't fight in open warfare, but used tactics like <u>sudden raids</u> and <u>ambushes</u>. They didn't wear uniforms and often operated in small groups.
4) American troops <u>weren't used</u> to fighting in the jungle.
5) The North Vietnamese had the <u>support</u> of China and the USSR.
6) American <u>public opinion</u> had turned against the war.

Vietnam — apocalypse then...
The <u>domino theory</u> explains why the USA thought Vietnam was so important, so learn it now.

Revision Summary

Yes, it's time for those awesome revision questions again — I know it's a pain but there's no way round it. It's the best way to test yourself on this stuff. So if you want to get the grades, you've really got to put the work in now. An important thing to remember here is that the USA and USSR were the only countries who were strong enough to have a major influence on world affairs after the Second World War — everybody else was too busy rebuilding their economies and industry. Make sure you can answer all of these lovely questions — and if you have problems go back over the section until you've got the lot sorted. So get going.

1) Name the two conferences held by the Big Three in 1945.
2) Which political leader was present at both of these conferences?
3) Was the USSR capitalist or communist?
4) Describe the difference between capitalism and communism.
5) Where and when did the USA use its atomic bombs?
6) When did the USA develop a hydrogen bomb?
7) Explain how the USSR developed a sphere of influence in Eastern Europe.
8) Which Eastern European country was communist but not under the USSR's influence?
9) What phrase did Winston Churchill use to describe the separation of Western Europe from Eastern Europe?
10) What was the Marshall Plan?
11) What was the Truman Doctrine?
12) Why did disagreements occur over the administration of Berlin in 1948?
13) What was the Berlin Blockade, and how did the Western powers deal with it?
14) Name the military dictator who was overthrown in Cuba in 1959.
15) How did Castro set about reducing American influence in Cuba?
16) What is a U-2?
17) Why did the world almost face a nuclear war in 1962?
18) Why did American public opinion turn against the war in Vietnam?
19) Give six reasons why the Americans failed to win the Vietnam War.

The Hungarian Rising and the Berlin Wall

During the 50s and 60s, most of <u>Eastern Europe</u> was under the <u>indirect control</u> of the <u>USSR</u>.

Hungary was treated Differently after the war

1) After the war, the USSR helped put <u>Rákosi</u>, a brutal Stalinist, in charge of Hungary. His <u>authoritarian</u> regime became increasingly unpopular.
2) In October 1956, the people of Budapest <u>protested</u> against the government of Rákosi.
3) The <u>secret police</u>, who'd executed or imprisoned thousands of Hungarians, were <u>hunted down</u>.
4) The Russian leader Khrushchev <u>allowed</u> the liberal Nagy to become Hungarian <u>Prime Minister</u>.
5) <u>Austria</u> (which borders on Hungary) declared itself a <u>neutral state</u> in 1955. Nagy hoped that Hungary could also be a <u>neutral state</u>.

In November 1956 Nagy announced that Hungary would <u>withdraw</u> from the Warsaw Pact and hold free elections — <u>ending communism</u> there.

Soviet Tanks Invaded Hungary

1) 20 000 Hungarians were <u>killed</u> or <u>wounded</u>.
2) Nagy was <u>arrested</u> and later <u>hanged</u>.
3) Kádár became Prime Minister and <u>ensured loyalty</u> towards the USSR.
4) Western countries <u>didn't</u> come to Hungary's aid.
5) When <u>Khrushchev</u> first came to power he seemed less harsh than <u>Stalin</u> — there was a "<u>thaw</u>" in the Cold War. But the response to the Hungarian Rising showed he could be <u>tough</u>.

The Berlin Wall was built in 1961

1) In 1949, Stalin ended the <u>Berlin Blockade</u> (see p.21). <u>Two new states</u> were formed — West Germany (German Federal Republic) and communist East Germany (German Democratic Republic).

2) Between 1949 and 1961, more than 2½ million people <u>left East Germany</u> for the West through East Berlin. The communist government of East Germany was <u>worried</u> by this trend.
3) So, on 13 August 1961, a 30-mile <u>barrier</u> was built across the city of Berlin overnight. The Berlin Wall was fortified with <u>barbed wire</u> and <u>machine gun</u> posts, and separated East Berlin from West Berlin.
4) Anyone who tried to <u>escape</u> East Berlin was <u>shot</u>. West Berliners were suddenly <u>separated</u> from relatives in the East — for the next 30 years.

In a famous speech in West Berlin on 26 June 1963, US President Kennedy declared his commitment to <u>protect</u> West Berlin, and his <u>solidarity</u> with its people. Kennedy said, "<u>Ich bin ein Berliner</u>" (I am a Berliner).

Things got better — then worse again...

OK, there are lots of facts here — the <u>key fact</u> you need to remember is that, even after Stalin's death, the USSR still wanted to <u>keep control</u> of Eastern Europe, even if they had to use <u>force</u>.

Czechoslovakia and Poland

The USSR's control of Eastern Europe faced some challenges.

Czechoslovakia Rebelled against Communism in 1968

1) Alexander Dubcek became Czechoslovakian leader in 1968 and made changes to the country:
   - Workers were given a greater say in the running of their factories.
   - Travel to the West was made available for all.
   - Living standards were to be raised.
   - Free elections were to be held.
   - Opposition parties would be permitted.

   This was called the 'Prague Spring'.

2) Dubcek was still a communist. He was careful to reassure the USSR that Czechoslovakia wouldn't leave the Warsaw Pact — unlike Hungary in 1956.

3) But the USSR was worried — it didn't want the Eastern Bloc to be weakened.

4) On 21st August 1968, 500 000 Soviet troops invaded Czechoslovakia and Dubcek was removed from office. Soviet control was restored. Many countries criticised the Soviets, but no action was taken. A UN draft resolution condemning the invasion was vetoed by the USSR.

5) Soviet leader Brezhnev (who replaced Khrushchev in 1964) said that in future the USSR would intervene in nations where socialism was under threat. This was called the Brezhnev Doctrine.

Poland's People Rebelled in 1980

1) In the late 1970s the economy in Poland suffered from foreign debt and shortages. In response the communist government raised prices.

2) In 1980 Lech Walesa led shipyard workers in the port of Gdansk in protest against the increase in food prices — with some success.

3) They set up their own independent trade union called 'Solidarity' and demanded the right to strike and to be consulted on all major decisions affecting their living and working conditions. Lech Walesa became the leader.

4) Solidarity became a broad-based anti-communist social movement which by the end of 1981 had 9 million members. Nothing like it had been seen before in the communist world. The movement was especially strong because of the support of the Catholic Church.

5) The Polish communist government was in a fix. It was scared to ban Solidarity — but neither could it meet demands for political reform, for fear of Soviet intervention.

The Military seized Control

In 1981 the Polish army leader General Jaruzelski, with Soviet support, seized control of the country and declared martial law. As a result:

1) Solidarity was completely banned.
2) Lech Walesa was arrested and imprisoned.
3) The price of basic foodstuffs was increased by 40%.

Solidarity lived on as an underground organisation. Lech Walesa became a symbol of resistance to Soviet oppression — he was awarded the Nobel Peace Prize in 1983. In 1988 further nationwide strikes again forced the government to negotiate with the union.

Solidarity — Rebels with a Cause...

Resistance to communism in Eastern Europe would eventually lead to the fall of the USSR.

The Soviet Withdrawal

Mikhail Gorbachev came to power in the USSR — and radically changed Soviet policies...

The Cold War created a Crisis in the USSR

1) The arms race with the USA was so expensive that Soviet living standards became worse as more money was spent on weapons.
2) Soviet farming was inefficient — there wasn't enough food and millions of tonnes of grain had to be imported from the USA.
3) The communist government was becoming more corrupt and was unable to give the Soviet people the same high living standards as people had in the West.
4) The USSR had been at war with Afghanistan since 1979. The war was a disaster — it cost billions of dollars and 15 000 Soviet troops were killed.

Gorbachev introduced Reforms

In 1985 Mikhail Gorbachev became General Secretary of the Communist Party. He was more open to the West than previous leaders. He introduced two major new policies — Glasnost and Perestroika.

Glasnost meant New Freedom and Openness

The Soviet people won new rights:
1) Thousands of political prisoners were released, including the leading dissident, Andrei Sakharov.
2) People were told about the atrocities committed by Stalin's government.
3) Free speech was allowed.
4) Military conscription was soon to be abolished.

Perestroika meant Economic Restructuring

1) Gorbachev wanted to make the Soviet system of central planning of production more efficient.
2) However corruption in the Soviet economy was too great and he was unable to see through his plans.

Gorbachev changed Foreign Policy

Gorbachev

1) In 1987, a disarmament treaty was signed called the INF (Intermediate-Range Nuclear Forces Treaty). The USA and the USSR agreed to remove medium-range nuclear missiles from Europe within three years.
2) In 1988, Gorbachev announced the immediate reduction of the weapons stockpile and the number of troops in the Soviet armed forces.
3) Gorbachev tried to improve relations with the West. He met with the US President Reagan several times, for example at the Geneva Summit in 1985.
4) Gorbachev announced the complete withdrawal of Soviet troops from Afghanistan in 1988.

In 1988, Gorbachev decided to abandon the Brezhnev Doctrine (see p.26). He told the United Nations that the countries of Eastern Europe now had a choice — the USSR wasn't going to control them any more.

It's feeling a bit less chilly in here...

By the late 1980s, the end of the Cold War was in sight. Don't forget — the attitude and leadership of Mikhail Gorbachev are the key to understanding why the situation changed.

The End of the Soviet Union

Communism toppled — and the Cold War was <u>finally over</u>...

Communism Fell all over Eastern Europe in 1989

1) Hungary <u>opened</u> its frontier with Austria in May.
2) <u>Free elections</u> were held in Poland in June. Solidarity won and a new non-communist government came to power.
3) Many <u>East</u> Germans <u>crossed</u> into Hungary, through Austria and into <u>West</u> Germany.
4) The <u>Berlin Wall</u> was <u>torn down</u> in November.
5) Anti-communist <u>demonstrations</u> took place in Czechoslovakia and the communist government <u>collapsed</u> in December.
6) In December a <u>revolution</u> began in Romania against the cruel and corrupt regime, and the dictator Nicolae Ceausescu was <u>executed</u> on Christmas Day.
7) The Warsaw Pact <u>ended</u> officially in <u>1991</u>.

In 1990 <u>Germany</u> was <u>reunified</u>. Communist East Germany and democratic West Germany were <u>one country</u> again after 45 years. For many people this was a powerful symbol that the communist experiment was over.

Communism was Rejected in the USSR

The main nationalities within the Soviet Union <u>demanded independence</u>, especially the Baltic republics — Latvia, Lithuania, and Estonia. Gorbachev tried to <u>prevent</u> the rise of nationalism in the Baltic republics with military force, but gradually started to <u>lose control</u>.

An Anti-Communist Russian President was Elected in 1991

1) The newly elected President of Russia, <u>Boris Yeltsin</u>, was an <u>opponent</u> of Gorbachev, and became <u>popular</u> and <u>powerful</u>.
2) He demanded the <u>end</u> of communist domination and the <u>break-up</u> of the USSR. This led to a <u>crisis</u> in 1991.

The Attempted Coup of 1991 Failed

1) The old communist leaders <u>feared</u> the reforms, so they decided to <u>get rid</u> of Gorbachev.
2) A military group tried to <u>seize power</u> by capturing Gorbachev, but Yeltsin rallied the Russian people to <u>resist</u> and the army supported him, and the coup <u>failed</u>.
3) Soon the individual Soviet republics became <u>independent</u> — the USSR didn't exist any more.
4) Now Gorbachev had no power and had to <u>resign</u>. Communism in Russia was dead.

The end of communism — when the reds got the blues...

Phew, there's even more stuff to learn here — but you've got to do it. Scribble a paragraph on why <u>communism fell</u> in Russia, and why <u>1991</u> was so important.

Terrorism

History didn't stop with the Cold War. Some current world issues are rapidly finding their way into the history books — including <u>terrorism</u>.

Terrorists use Fear to make a Political Point

1) Terrorism is the use of <u>fear</u> to achieve <u>political goals</u>. Terrorists use tactics such as <u>bombing</u> public places, taking <u>hostages</u> and <u>hijacking</u> aeroplanes.
2) It's usually <u>condemned</u> because it puts <u>innocent civilians</u> in danger.
3) Terrorists often claim that they use violence because they have <u>no choice</u>. They say it's the only way to get their <u>voice heard</u> — e.g. in a non-democratic state.
4) Sometimes a group is called "<u>terrorists</u>" by some people and "<u>freedom fighters</u>" by others. It all depends <u>how sympathetic</u> you are to what they're trying to achieve and on your views of their methods.
5) Terror networks are now <u>international</u>. Terrorist organisations trade with each other for <u>weapons</u> and <u>training</u>. Some terrorist groups receive money from <u>governments</u> who want to harm other countries without being held responsible.

The IRA wanted Ireland to be United

Northern Ireland (mainly Protestant)

Eire (mainly Catholic)

1) In 1921, Ireland was <u>divided</u> into <u>Eire</u> (the Catholic, southern part of the country) and <u>Northern Ireland</u> (the mainly Protestant northern area), which stayed part of the United Kingdom.
2) The <u>Protestant</u> majority living in the North <u>discriminated</u> against Catholics, for example in jobs and housing. In <u>1969</u> violence broke out in Northern Ireland over <u>civil rights</u> for <u>Catholics</u>.
3) The <u>Provisional IRA (Irish Republican Army)</u> wanted Northern Ireland to be united with Eire. They used <u>terrorist tactics</u>.
4) A long period of serious violence was known as the <u>Troubles</u> (1969-1998). <u>Over 3000 people were killed</u> and many more were injured on both sides of the conflict.
5) There were <u>revenge killings</u> between the IRA and its opponents — the "loyalist" <u>UVF</u> (Ulster Volunteer Force) and <u>UDA</u> (Ulster Defence Association).
6) The IRA wanted to <u>wear down</u> the British government so they would eventually decide that defending Northern Ireland wasn't <u>worth the cost</u> in lives and resources.

Key events during the 'Troubles'

- From <u>1971</u> the IRA began <u>killing British soldiers</u>, including 100 British soldiers in <u>1972</u>.
- The IRA started bombing <u>commercial targets</u>, e.g. <u>Belfast city centre</u> in <u>1972</u>.
- In <u>1973</u> the bombing spread to <u>England</u>. In 1974, there were <u>pub bombings</u> in <u>Guildford</u> and <u>Birmingham</u>. The <u>Brighton hotel bombing</u> in <u>1984</u> was an attempt to kill Margaret Thatcher.
- In <u>1997</u> the IRA agreed to a <u>ceasefire</u>.
- In <u>1998</u>, the British and Irish governments, and most Northern Ireland political parties, including <u>Sinn Fein</u> (associated with the IRA), signed the <u>Good Friday Agreement</u>. It was a move towards <u>power-sharing</u> in Northern Ireland through new political bodies such as a <u>Northern Ireland Assembly</u>. It also included plans for the <u>decommissioning</u> of <u>weapons</u> by paramilitary groups, and a commitment to use only <u>democratic</u> and <u>peaceful</u> methods.

The Troubles were troubling times...

Terrorism and violence created a climate of fear in Northern Ireland during the 'Troubles'. In the end it was <u>peaceful negotiation</u> and the 'Good Friday Agreement' that helped to bring progress.

Terrorism

Some terrorists are willing to negotiate, but extreme organisations tend to rely on violence alone.

The PLO used both Terrorist Tactics and Diplomacy

Yasser Arafat

1) Israel was created in 1948 as a homeland for Jewish people after World War 2. The region had historical and cultural significance for Jews. However, there was conflict between the Jewish settlers and Palestinian Arabs who lived in the region. 750 000 Palestinians became refugees.
2) The Palestine Liberation Organisation (PLO) was created in 1964 by Arab nationalists who wanted to win Palestine back from Israel. Yasser Arafat became the chairman of the PLO in 1969. He was a strong leader.
3) The PLO was made up of different groups. Arafat belonged to Fatah — the largest group, which was relatively moderate. Other groups were more extreme.
4) The PLO used terrorist tactics, e.g. the 1978 Coastal Road Massacre killed 38 Israelis, including 13 Israeli children.
5) But it also wanted to be accepted as the representative of the Palestinian people.
6) Like the IRA, the PLO eventually reduced its demands. In 1988 it agreed to a two-state solution which would divide Palestine into separate Jewish and Arab states.
7) In the Oslo Accords (1993) the Israeli government recognised the PLO as the legitimate representative of the Palestinians. The PLO recognised that Israel had a right to exist in peace. Arafat became President of the new Palestinian Authority which controlled some of the territory previously occupied by Israel.

Al-Qaeda is an International terrorist organisation

1) Al-Qaeda is a global terrorist network with extreme Islamic views. Its members want to create a unified Muslim nation with strict religious laws and no Western influences.
2) Its founder was Osama bin Laden, a Saudi Arabian. During the 1990s, the Taliban regime in Afghanistan supported al-Qaeda and allowed them to build training camps for terrorists.
3) "Jihad" is the Islamic idea of a "spiritual struggle" but some terrorists use it to mean "holy war". In 1996 al-Qaeda announced a jihad to remove foreign troops from Islamic lands.
4) In 1998 bin Laden announced that it was the duty of every Muslim to kill Americans.

The Khobar Towers bombing in Saudi Arabia in 1996 was aimed at US servicemen (19 died). The East African US Embassy bombings in 1998 killed about 200 people, mostly locals.

Al-Qaeda attacked the World Trade Center in New York and the Pentagon in Washington on 11 September 2001. The attack destroyed the twin towers and killed around 3000 people. It was the worst terrorist attack in history. In response, the USA declared a "war on terror" and invaded Afghanistan. They destroyed many terrorist training camps but bin Laden wasn't captured.

Even though Osama bin Laden went into hiding, the attacks continued, e.g. the Bali nightclub bombings in 2002 and many suicide bombings in Iraq.

5) Bin Laden was eventually tracked down and killed in Pakistan by a US military raid in 2011.

Not all terrorist groups are willing to negotiate...

The IRA and PLO used violent tactics but eventually they were willing to negotiate in a peace process. Extreme terrorist groups like Al-Qaeda don't use diplomacy and won't compromise. They rely on high profile attacks to make headlines and promote their cause.

The Iraq War

The decision to invade Iraq in 2003 was extremely <u>controversial</u>...

The First Gulf War was in 1990-1991

1) Iraq is made up of different ethnic groups. It's mainly <u>Arab</u>, but there's a strong <u>Kurdish minority</u> (17%) in the North. The main religion is Islam, which in Iraq is divided into a <u>Shi'ite majority</u> and a <u>Sunni minority</u>.
2) <u>Saddam Hussein</u> came to power in 1979. His <u>Ba'ath Party</u> was socialist and secular (non-religious), but his rule <u>favoured the Sunni minority</u>.
3) The USA <u>supported</u> Iraq during its war with Iran in the <u>1980s</u>.
4) But after <u>Iraq invaded Kuwait in 1990</u> President Bush (George W. Bush's father) led international forces against Saddam Hussein in the <u>First Gulf War</u>.

George Bush

George W Bush wanted to Remove Saddam from Power

When <u>George W Bush</u> became US President in 2001, he wanted to invade Iraq. He claimed that Saddam had links to <u>al-Qaeda</u> and was developing <u>weapons of mass destruction</u>.

In October 2002 Congress passed the <u>Iraq War Resolution</u>. This made the invasion of Iraq legal because it hadn't met the conditions of the 1991 <u>ceasefire</u>. Congress accused Iraq of developing <u>weapons of mass destruction</u> (WMD), <u>protecting terrorists</u> and acts of <u>brutality</u>.

In November 2002 the <u>UN Security Council</u> passed <u>Resolution 1441</u>, giving Iraq a <u>final chance</u> to give up its weapons, but Iraq didn't comply. Some people argue that the case should have gone back to the UN because Resolution 1441 <u>did not authorise</u> the invasion.

In March 2003, the US <u>invaded</u> Iraq. British Prime Minister <u>Tony Blair</u> supported US policy and <u>Britain</u> became America's main <u>ally</u> in the war.

It turned out there weren't any WMD

After the invasion, it became clear that there was <u>no evidence</u> of <u>WMD</u> or links to <u>al-Qaeda</u>. This was embarrassing for the USA so they put forward other arguments for the invasion:
1) Getting rid of a dictator and establishing <u>democracy</u> could be seen as <u>progress</u> for Iraq.
2) The war was justified by <u>Saddam's appalling human rights record</u>.

Millions Demonstrated Against the War

There were anti-war <u>protests</u> involving millions of people in early 2003.

Some people didn't trust the USA's motives for war — they thought that the US wanted Iraq's oil supply and lied about the WMD.

Others felt uneasy about Western nations invading Iraq. Iraq had once been controlled by the British Empire — there were echoes of colonialism.

The idea of these Western, mainly Christian countries invading a Muslim country made some people feel uncomfortable.

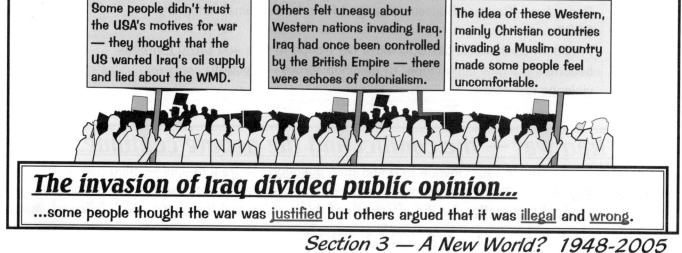

The invasion of Iraq divided public opinion...

...some people thought the war was <u>justified</u> but others argued that it was <u>illegal</u> and <u>wrong</u>.

The Iraq War

The invasion was fairly <u>quick</u> and <u>easy</u>, but the conflict went on <u>longer</u> than anyone expected.

Saddam's regime Crumbled in just over a Month...

1) In <u>March 2003</u>, <u>coalition forces</u> led by the US <u>invaded Iraq</u>.
2) They captured the capital <u>Baghdad</u> on <u>9 April</u>. The coalition had about 200 000 ground troops who were <u>far better equipped</u> than the Iraqis, and had total <u>air superiority</u>.
3) On <u>1 May</u> President <u>Bush</u> announced US <u>victory</u> in Iraq.

...but the Conflict went on

Saddam Hussein

1) After Saddam's defeat, there was widespread <u>looting</u> and <u>civil disorder</u>. The coalition forces lacked the <u>manpower</u> to deal with the problem.
2) Many members of the defeated Iraqi Army became <u>insurgents</u> (resisting the invasion). They used weapons supplied by <u>terrorists</u>.
3) <u>Saddam Hussein</u> went into hiding but was <u>captured</u> in December 2003.
4) In <u>2004</u> resistance to the US coalition <u>increased</u>, helped by foreign fighters and al-Qaeda. Fighting included a 46-day battle for the city of <u>Fallujah</u> starting in <u>November 2004</u>. It was eventually <u>won</u> by US forces.
5) Over the next few years, 2 million Iraqis <u>fled</u> the country to escape the war. Some Iraqis were angry that the coalition couldn't <u>protect civilians</u>.
6) <u>US soldiers</u> were found guilty of <u>abusing prisoners</u> at <u>Abu Ghraib</u> prison in April 2004. This was a major blow to the <u>moral justification</u> for invading Iraq.

Achieving Democracy and Security was a Slow Process

Coalition forces tried to <u>improve security</u> but there was still some <u>resistance</u>.

2005
January – Iraqis elect a <u>transitional government</u> — many Sunnis refuse to vote
May – Sunni <u>suicide bombers</u> kill hundreds of Shias
October – a referendum approves the new Iraqi <u>constitution</u>
December – a <u>national assembly</u> is elected with Sunnis and Shias
2006
February – Sunnis bomb a Shia <u>holy site</u>, the al-Askari mosque
May – new Iraqi <u>government</u> takes office
November – <u>violence</u> increases, hundreds killed in Baghdad
December – Saddam Hussein is <u>hanged</u> for crimes against humanity
2007
President Bush sends 20 000 extra US troops to Iraq and <u>David Petraeus</u> becomes the new commander of coalition forces — <u>security</u> improves, <u>violence</u> decreases

The Iraq war — the conflict and the debate continue...

Coalition forces couldn't just invade Iraq and then <u>abandon</u> the Iraqi people — they had a <u>responsibility</u> to leave the country in a stable condition. People who oppose the war <u>criticise</u> the US for its <u>lack of preparation</u> for the aftermath of the invasion and the <u>chaos</u> which followed.

Revision Summary

There's just time for the best bit — some mega-magnificent revision questions for you. You've really got to test yourself here, because there were loads of facts. See how many you can answer first go, then look back over the areas you weren't so sure about. Just keep coming back to those questions — by the time you sit the exam you should know them backwards... Well, forwards will do. So get busy and get this lot sorted.

1) Why did Soviet tanks invade Hungary in 1956?

2) When was the Berlin Wall built?

3) What was the Prague Spring?

4) Who was the leader of the Solidarity movement in Poland?

5) When was Mikhail Gorbachev appointed General Secretary of the Soviet Union's Communist Party?

6) Explain what is meant by the terms Glasnost and Perestroika.

7) Why was Perestroika unsuccessful?

8) What was agreed in the INF treaty?

9) What doctrine did Gorbachev abandon in 1988?

10) What year was the Berlin Wall torn down?

11) What year was Germany reunified?

12) What happened to Romanian dictator Nicolae Ceausescu in 1989?

13) What was the name of the President of Russia elected in 1991?

14) Briefly describe the events of the attempted coup against Gorbachev in 1991.

15) Give three examples of terrorist tactics.

16) Which area of Ireland is mainly Catholic and which is mainly Protestant?

17) Name the terrorist group that wanted Northern Ireland to be united with Eire.

18) What were 'The Troubles'?

19) What is the name of the Northern Ireland peace process agreement signed in 1998?

20) What does PLO stand for?

21) Who was made leader of the PLO in 1969?

22) What was agreed in the Oslo Accords?

23) What is the main aim of al-Qaeda?

24) Name three terrorist attacks carried out by al-Qaeda.

25) What did the Iraq War Resolution do?

26) What was Resolution 1441?

27) Give three reasons why some people opposed the war in Iraq.

28) When did US coalition forces invade Iraq and what date did President Bush claim victory?

29) When was Saddam Hussein captured?

30) What crime happened at Abu Ghraib prison?

The Weimar Republic

Germany lost the First World War (1914-1918). The peace settlement was harsh on Germany — it said Germany should accept blame for the war and pay £6.6 billion reparations.

A New Government Took Over When the Kaiser Abdicated

1) Kaiser Wilhelm II had ruled the German Empire as a monarch. At the end of the First World War there was a period of violent unrest in Germany — and the Kaiser was forced to abdicate in November 1918.
2) In early 1919, a new government took power led by Friedrich Ebert — it changed Germany into a republic. It was set up in Weimar, because there was violence in Berlin. Ebert became the first President, with Scheidemann as Chancellor.
3) Ebert was leader of the Social Democratic Party, a moderate party of socialists. The new government was democratic — they believed the people should say how the country was run.
4) The new German government wasn't invited to the peace conference in 1919 — and had no say in the Versailles Treaty. At first, Ebert refused to sign the treaty, but in the end he had little choice — Germany was too weak to risk restarting the conflict.

The Weimar Constitution made Germany a Republic

THE WEIMAR GOVERNMENT

REICHSRAT (Upper house — could delay measures passed by Reichstag).

REICHSTAG The new German parliament (elected by proportional representation).

PRESIDENT Elected every 7 years. Head of army. Chooses the Chancellor.

Friedrich Ebert

Proportional representation is where the number of seats a party wins in parliament is worked out as a proportion of the number of votes they win. This was the system in Germany and it often led to lots of political parties in the Reichstag (German parliament) — making it harder to get laws passed.

The Weimar Republic had Many Problems

1) It was difficult to make decisions because there were so many parties in the Reichstag.
2) It was hard to pick a Chancellor who had the support of most of the Reichstag.
3) The new government had to accept the Versailles Treaty, so they were hated by many Germans because of the territory loss, the 'war guilt' clause, the reparations etc. (see p.3).

4) Some Germans joined paramilitary groups, such as the Freikorps (Free Corps) — right-wing groups made up of ex-soldiers who saw communists as a threat to peace.
5) Even though the Freikorps were problematic — they were private organisations not under government control — Ebert was happy to use them to suppress communist uprisings.

Weimar — not a kind of sausage...

The Weimar Republic was set up in a time of defeat — which made it unpopular right from the start. Don't forget — many German people didn't accept the peace settlements at the end of the First World War. Scribble a quick paragraph on the Weimar Republic and how it was set up.

The Years of Unrest

Germany faced all sorts of <u>problems</u> in the years following the First World War.

Reasons for Discontent

1) Thousands of people were <u>poor</u> and <u>starving</u>. An <u>influenza</u> epidemic had killed thousands.
2) Many Germans <u>denied</u> they had lost the war and blamed the <u>'November Criminals'</u> who had agreed to the Armistice and the Treaty of Versailles.
3) Others <u>blamed</u> for losing the war included the communists, the government and the Jews.
4) The government was seen as <u>weak</u> and <u>ineffective</u> — the <u>Treaty of Versailles</u> had made living conditions <u>worse</u> in Germany.

Soon there were <u>Riots</u> and <u>Rebellions</u>

1) In 1919, the <u>communists</u> led by Karl Liebknecht and Rosa Luxemburg tried to <u>take over</u> Berlin in the <u>Spartacist Revolt</u> — but they were defeated by the Freikorps.

Wolfgang Kapp

2) In 1920, some of the right-wing Freikorps themselves took part in the Kapp Putsch (Putsch means revolt) — led by Wolfgang Kapp, they <u>took over</u> Berlin to form another government. The workers staged a General Strike — Kapp <u>gave up</u>. The government <u>didn't</u> punish the rebels, because many judges <u>sympathised</u> with people like Kapp.

3) In 1922 Walter Rathenau was <u>assassinated</u> — he was the Foreign Minister who <u>signed</u> a peace treaty with Russia after the war, and was <u>Jewish</u>. Many Germans were now anti-Jewish (<u>anti-Semitic</u>).

In 1923 <u>Germany Couldn't Pay</u> the Reparations

France and Belgium occupied the Ruhr — the <u>richest</u> industrial part of Germany — to <u>take resources</u> instead. This led to fury in Germany, while workers in the Ruhr <u>refused</u> to work. German industry was devastated again, plunging the economy into <u>hyperinflation</u>.

1918	Aug 1923	Nov 1923
Egg =	1/4 Mark	5000 Marks	80 million Marks

HYPERINFLATION - THE PRICE OF AN EGG IN GERMANY

<u>Hyperinflation</u> happens when production can't keep up with the amount of money there is, so the <u>money</u> keeps <u>losing its value</u>.

Hyperinflation had Three Major Results

1) <u>Wages</u> were paid <u>twice a day</u> before prices went up again.
2) The middle classes lost out as <u>bank savings</u> became <u>worthless</u>.
3) The German <u>Mark</u> became <u>worthless</u>.

Hyperinflation — sounds good for blowing up balloons...

Remember that discontent in Germany got <u>worse</u> when the economy <u>went wrong</u> — but there were lots of other factors too. Scribble a list of <u>reasons</u> why there was so much discontent.

Stresemann and Recovery

In August 1923 Stresemann became Chancellor — he gradually led Germany back to <u>recovery</u>.

Stresemann <u>wanted</u> International Cooperation

Stresemann was Chancellor for a few months, then Foreign Minister. He believed Germany's <u>best chance</u> for recovery came from working with <u>other countries</u>.

1) In September 1923 he told the workers in the Ruhr to <u>return</u> to work.
2) He <u>accepted</u> the Dawes Plan in 1924, and <u>introduced</u> a <u>new</u> German Mark called the <u>Rentenmark</u> to make the currency more stable.
3) In 1925 the French and Belgian <u>troops left</u> the Ruhr.
4) In October 1925 he <u>agreed</u> to the <u>Locarno Treaty</u> where the western borders of Germany were agreed, but not the eastern. He won the <u>Nobel Peace Prize</u> for his efforts in this field.
5) In 1926, Germany <u>joined</u> the League of Nations, and became one of the permanent members of the Council.
6) In 1928, Germany was one of <u>65 countries</u> to sign the <u>Kellogg-Briand Pact</u>. They promised <u>not to use violence</u> to settle disputes.
7) In 1929, the Young Plan <u>replaced</u> the Dawes Plan — <u>reparations</u> would be <u>reduced</u> by three-quarters of the amount, and Germany was given 59 years to pay them.

USA

Britain & France pay back debts to USA

Lends money to Germany

Germany pays back France and Britain (Reparations)

The Dawes Plan

Germany had Begun to Recover — but Depended on US Money

Gustav Stresemann

Life was beginning to <u>look better</u> for Germany thanks to the work of Stresemann. But he <u>died</u> in October <u>1929</u>, just before the disaster of the <u>Wall Street Crash</u> (see p.70). The plans he had agreed would only work if the <u>USA</u> had <u>enough money</u> to keep lending to Germany — but now it didn't. Things were suddenly going to <u>get worse again</u>.

The Weimar Republic had many Cultural Achievements

1) Germany's capital <u>Berlin</u> became a <u>centre for culture</u> under the Weimar Republic.
2) There were advances in <u>art</u>, <u>architecture</u>, <u>music</u> and <u>literature</u>. German films were successful — e.g. 'Metropolis', directed by <u>Fritz Lang</u>.
3) Some developments were <u>bold</u> and <u>new</u>, like the drama of <u>Bertolt Brecht</u>. The <u>Bauhaus School</u> of <u>design</u> was highly influential.
4) The Weimar Republic encouraged new ways of <u>critical thinking</u> at places like <u>Frankfurt University</u>.
5) Not everyone approved of these cultural changes — the <u>cabaret culture</u> in Berlin was seen as <u>immoral</u> by some. The culture of the Weimar Republic <u>didn't survive</u> under the <u>Nazis</u>...

It was nearly all okay...

The 1920s were a tough decade in Germany, but Stresemann seemed to have the problems sorted. Scribble a paragraph on the work of <u>Stresemann</u> — his policies at home and abroad.

The Roots of the Nazi Party

The Nazi Party was a small organisation in the 1920s — but it had big ambitions...

Adolf Hitler was the Nazi Leader

1) Born in Austria in 1889, Hitler had lived in Germany from 1912 onwards.
2) He'd been a brave soldier on the Western Front in World War I, winning the Iron Cross twice. He couldn't accept that Germany had lost the war.
3) In 1919, he joined the German Workers' Party, led by Anton Drexler. It was a tiny party — Hitler was the 55th member. In 1920 the name was changed to the National Socialist German Workers' Party (Nazis).
4) Hitler was a charismatic speaker and attracted new members. He took over the leadership of the party.
5) The party set up its own armed group called the SA — brown-shirted stormtroopers who protected Nazi leaders and harassed their opponents.

Hitler tried to Overthrow the Government in the Munich Putsch

1) In 1923, things were going badly for the Weimar Republic — it seemed weak.
2) Hitler planned to overthrow the Weimar government — starting by taking control of the government in a region called Bavaria.
3) Hitler's soldiers occupied a beer hall in the Bavarian city of Munich where local government leaders were meeting. He announced that the revolution had begun.
4) The next day Hitler marched into Munich supported by stormtroopers. But the revolt quickly collapsed when police fired on the rebels.

Hitler wrote the book 'Mein Kampf' in Prison

1) Hitler was imprisoned for his role in the Munich Putsch.
2) He wrote a book in prison describing his beliefs and ambitions. The title 'Mein Kampf' means 'My Struggle'.

Believed ARYAN races were MASTER RACE
(He meant Northern European people, but got it wrong)

Would join Austria and Germany (Anschluss)

Would reverse Versailles Treaty

Would create a greater Germany

Germans had a right to LEBENSRAUM (more space to live)

He believed other races were inferior

After the Munich Putsch Hitler Changed Tactics

1) The Nazi party was banned after the Munich Putsch. After Hitler was released from prison, he re-established the party with himself as supreme leader.
2) By the mid-1920s, the German economy was starting to recover under Stresemann. As a result, general support for the Nazis declined and overturning the government through a coup no longer seemed realistic.
3) Hitler changed tactics — he now tried to gain control through the democratic system. The Nazi party network was extended nationally, instead of it being a regional party. Propaganda was used to promote the party's beliefs.

The Nazis — ready to sweep to power...

Very few people supported the Nazis at this stage. There were fewer than 30 000 members by 1925, and in the 1928 elections the Nazis had 12 Reichstag members, compared with 54 communists and 153 Social Democrats. All that was about to change though...

The Rise of the Nazis

The Depression hit Germany hard. The popularity of the Nazi Party soared as a result — people thought the Weimar government couldn't sort out Germany's problems.

The Great Depression caused Poverty and Suffering

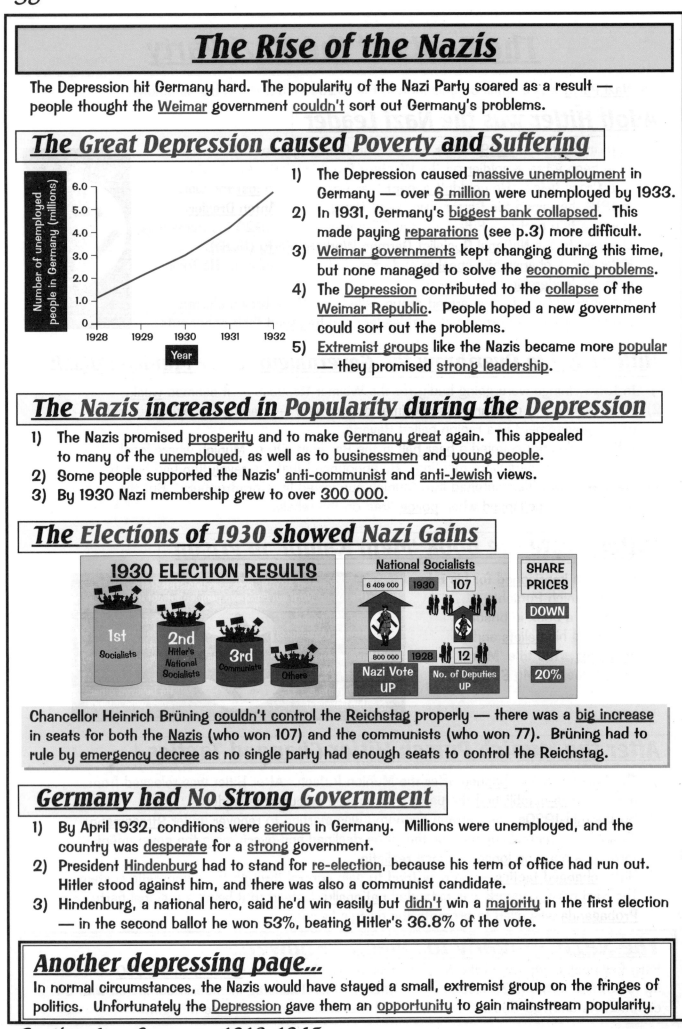

1) The Depression caused massive unemployment in Germany — over 6 million were unemployed by 1933.
2) In 1931, Germany's biggest bank collapsed. This made paying reparations (see p.3) more difficult.
3) Weimar governments kept changing during this time, but none managed to solve the economic problems.
4) The Depression contributed to the collapse of the Weimar Republic. People hoped a new government could sort out the problems.
5) Extremist groups like the Nazis became more popular — they promised strong leadership.

The Nazis increased in Popularity during the Depression

1) The Nazis promised prosperity and to make Germany great again. This appealed to many of the unemployed, as well as to businessmen and young people.
2) Some people supported the Nazis' anti-communist and anti-Jewish views.
3) By 1930 Nazi membership grew to over 300 000.

The Elections of 1930 showed Nazi Gains

1930 ELECTION RESULTS

1st Socialists
2nd Hitler's National Socialists
3rd Communists
Others

National Socialists

6 409 000 | 1930 | 107

800 000 | 1928 | 12

Nazi Vote UP

No. of Deputies UP

SHARE PRICES

DOWN

20%

Chancellor Heinrich Brüning couldn't control the Reichstag properly — there was a big increase in seats for both the Nazis (who won 107) and the communists (who won 77). Brüning had to rule by emergency decree as no single party had enough seats to control the Reichstag.

Germany had No Strong Government

1) By April 1932, conditions were serious in Germany. Millions were unemployed, and the country was desperate for a strong government.
2) President Hindenburg had to stand for re-election, because his term of office had run out. Hitler stood against him, and there was also a communist candidate.
3) Hindenburg, a national hero, said he'd win easily but didn't win a majority in the first election — in the second ballot he won 53%, beating Hitler's 36.8% of the vote.

Another depressing page...

In normal circumstances, the Nazis would have stayed a small, extremist group on the fringes of politics. Unfortunately the Depression gave them an opportunity to gain mainstream popularity.

The Rise of the Nazis

The Nazis gained a lot of votes — but they used some underhand tactics to get them...

Hindenburg Refused to give the Nazis Power

1) Hindenburg couldn't find a Chancellor who had support in the Reichstag.
2) He appointed the inexperienced Franz von Papen.
3) In the July 1932 Reichstag elections, the Nazis won 230 seats — they were now the biggest party, but didn't have a majority in the Reichstag. Hitler demanded to be made Chancellor.
4) Hindenburg refused because he didn't trust Hitler and kept von Papen.

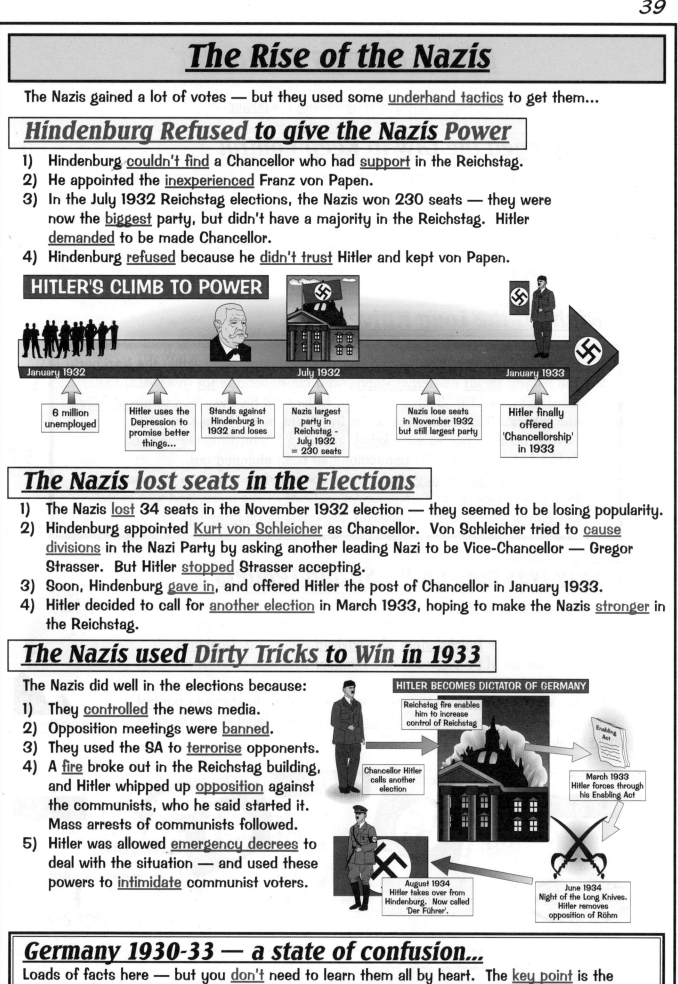

HITLER'S CLIMB TO POWER

January 1932 — July 1932 — January 1933

| 6 million unemployed | Hitler uses the Depression to promise better things... | Stands against Hindenburg in 1932 and loses | Nazis largest party in Reichstag - July 1932 = 230 seats | Nazis lose seats in November 1932 but still largest party | Hitler finally offered 'Chancellorship' in 1933 |

The Nazis lost seats in the Elections

1) The Nazis lost 34 seats in the November 1932 election — they seemed to be losing popularity.
2) Hindenburg appointed Kurt von Schleicher as Chancellor. Von Schleicher tried to cause divisions in the Nazi Party by asking another leading Nazi to be Vice-Chancellor — Gregor Strasser. But Hitler stopped Strasser accepting.
3) Soon, Hindenburg gave in, and offered Hitler the post of Chancellor in January 1933.
4) Hitler decided to call for another election in March 1933, hoping to make the Nazis stronger in the Reichstag.

The Nazis used Dirty Tricks to Win in 1933

The Nazis did well in the elections because:

1) They controlled the news media.
2) Opposition meetings were banned.
3) They used the SA to terrorise opponents.
4) A fire broke out in the Reichstag building, and Hitler whipped up opposition against the communists, who he said started it. Mass arrests of communists followed.
5) Hitler was allowed emergency decrees to deal with the situation — and used these powers to intimidate communist voters.

HITLER BECOMES DICTATOR OF GERMANY

Chancellor Hitler calls another election

Reichstag fire enables him to increase control of Reichstag

March 1933 Hitler forces through his Enabling Act

August 1934 Hitler takes over from Hindenburg. Now called 'Der Führer'.

June 1934 Night of the Long Knives. Hitler removes opposition of Röhm

Germany 1930-33 — a state of confusion...

Loads of facts here — but you don't need to learn them all by heart. The key point is the sequence of events. Hitler didn't come to power overnight — his support increased as the economy got worse and as the other political parties failed to solve Germany's problems.

Hitler Comes to Power

Once Hitler was Chancellor he set about strengthening his <u>power</u>...

Hitler Changed the Law to Keep Control

1) The Nazis won 288 seats but <u>no</u> majority — the communists still won 81.
2) So Hitler <u>declared</u> the Communist Party <u>illegal</u>.
3) This gave him enough <u>support</u> in parliament to bring in an <u>Enabling Bill</u> which was passed with threats and bargaining in March 1933.
4) This bill let him <u>govern</u> for four years <u>without</u> parliament and made all other parties illegal. Hitler was almost in full control.

The Night of the Long Knives

1) Hitler still had opposition — and was worried about <u>rivals</u> within the Nazi party.
2) The biggest <u>threat</u> was <u>Ernst Röhm</u>, who controlled the <u>SA</u> (over 400 000 men). On the 29th-30th June 1934, Hitler sent his own men to <u>arrest</u> Röhm and others. This became known as the 'Night of the Long Knives'.
3) Several hundred people were <u>killed</u>, including Röhm, Strasser and von Schleicher. Any potential <u>opposition</u> had been <u>stamped out</u>.
4) A month later <u>Hindenburg died</u>. Hitler combined the posts of Chancellor and President, made himself Commander-in-Chief of the army, and was called <u>Der Führer</u> (the leader). It was the beginning of <u>dictatorship</u>.

Germany was now under Strong Leaders

1) Germany was <u>reorganised</u> into a number of provinces. Each province was called a Gau (plural: Gaue), with a Gauleiter — a loyal Nazi — in charge of each.
2) Above them were the <u>Reichsleiters</u> who <u>advised</u> Hitler, e.g. <u>Goebbels</u> who was in charge of propaganda, and <u>Himmler</u> who was chief of the German police.
3) At the top was the <u>Führer</u> — Hitler himself — who was in absolute <u>control</u>.
4) Every aspect of life was carefully <u>controlled</u>, and only <u>loyal</u> Nazis could be <u>successful</u>.

Joseph Goebbels

Hitler was obsessed with power...

Once elected the Nazis pretty quickly turned Germany from a democracy into a <u>dictatorship</u>. Hitler set himself up as a <u>supreme ruler</u> — Chancellor, President and army chief combined.

Nazi Methods of Control

The Nazis used many methods to control the German people — from persuasion to <u>violence</u>...

The Nazis used <u>Propaganda</u>

<u>Propaganda</u> means spreading particular ideas and <u>points of view</u> to try to control how people think. Nazi propaganda blamed the <u>Jews</u> and <u>communists</u> for most of Germany's problems.

1) The Nazis took over the <u>media</u>. They controlled <u>radio broadcasts</u>, and also used <u>films</u> and <u>posters</u> to spread their messages.

2) The <u>Ministry of Public Enlightenment and Propaganda</u> (founded in <u>1933</u>) was led by <u>Dr Joseph Goebbels</u>. All artists, writers, journalists and musicians had to <u>register</u> to get their <u>work approved</u>.
3) The Nazis organised huge <u>rallies</u> of party members to present an <u>image</u> of power and popularity. They also used the <u>1936 Berlin Olympics</u> as an opportunity for <u>international publicity</u>.

The Nazis used <u>Censorship</u>

1) The Nazis <u>censored</u> books, newspapers and other material.
2) Those who published anti-Nazi material risked <u>execution</u>.
3) The Nazis used censorship to encourage <u>nationalism</u> and <u>anti-Semitism (hatred of Jews)</u>. They praised patriotic German composers such as <u>Wagner</u> but banned the work of Jewish composers such as Mendelssohn.

Germany became a <u>Police State</u>

1) The <u>SS</u> (<u>Schutzstaffel</u>) began as a bodyguard for Hitler. It expanded massively under the leadership of Himmler during the 1930s. Its members were totally loyal to Hitler, and were feared for their <u>cruelty</u>. Himmler was also in charge of the <u>secret police</u> — the <u>Gestapo</u>.
2) After 1933 <u>concentration camps</u> spread across Germany and its territories to hold political prisoners and anybody else considered dangerous to the Nazis. Some of these were later turned into <u>death camps</u> (see p.45).
3) Local <u>wardens</u> were employed to make sure Germans were loyal to the Nazis. People were encouraged to <u>report disloyalty</u>. Many were arrested by the Gestapo as a result.

The Nazis saw the Church as a <u>Threat</u>

1) Many Nazis were against Christianity — its teaching of <u>peace</u> was seen as incompatible with Nazi ideas. However, the Nazis didn't want to <u>risk</u> an immediate attack on it.
2) Hitler signed an <u>agreement</u> with the <u>Catholic Church</u> in 1933. Each side promised not to interfere with the other. However the Nazis did try to <u>curb</u> the influence of the church — and there were some Catholic <u>protests</u> against Nazi policies.
3) Hitler tried to unite the different Protestant churches into one Reich Church. He placed the Nazi Bishop Ludwig Müller at its head. Some church members split off in protest at this state interference. They formed the <u>Confessing Church</u> (see p.44).
4) Many clergy who stood up to the Nazi regime were sent to <u>concentration camps</u>.

This book wouldn't be available in Nazi Germany...

Imagine if the radio and newspapers all covered the <u>same news</u> in the same way, and featured all the <u>same opinions</u>. You might start to think that way after a while.

German Growth Under the Nazis

The Nazis took strict <u>control</u> of the economy.

Hitler gave Work to 6 Million Unemployed

1) Hitler started a huge <u>programme</u> of <u>public works</u>, which gave <u>jobs</u> to thousands of people.
2) From 1933, huge motorways — <u>Autobahns</u> — were started. <u>Unemployment fell</u> dramatically.
3) But — the Nazis also <u>fiddled with the statistics</u> to make unemployment look <u>lower</u> than it really was. E.g. they didn't count women or Jewish people in the unemployment statistics — this is called "<u>invisible unemployment</u>".

People were Encouraged to Work by Rewards

1) <u>All</u> men between 18 and 25 could be <u>recruited</u> into the <u>National Labour Service</u> and given jobs.
2) The Nazis got rid of trade unions. Instead workers had to join the Nazi's <u>Labour Front</u>.
3) The Nazis introduced '<u>Strength through Joy</u>' — a scheme which provided workers with <u>cheap holidays</u> and leisure activities. Another scheme, '<u>Beauty of Labour</u>', encouraged factory owners to <u>improve conditions</u> for their workers.
4) Output increased in Germany, and <u>unemployment</u> was almost <u>ended</u> completely. The Nazis introduced the <u>Volkswagen</u> (the people's car) as an <u>ambition</u> for people to aim for.
5) <u>Wages</u> were still relatively <u>low</u> though — and workers <u>weren't allowed</u> to go on <u>strike</u> or campaign for better conditions.

Hitler Re-armed the Germany Military

1) Another way to create work was to <u>build up</u> the armed forces. The Nazis did this <u>secretly</u> at first, because the <u>Treaty of Versailles</u> had <u>banned</u> it.
2) Hitler <u>sacked</u> some of the generals, and <u>replaced</u> them with Nazi supporters. Goering was put in charge of the newly-formed <u>Luftwaffe</u> (airforce), which had been banned at Versailles.
3) In 1935, <u>military conscription</u> was reintroduced (drafting men into the army).
4) In 1936, the Nazis introduced a <u>Four-Year Plan</u> to <u>prepare</u> the country for war. <u>Industrial production</u> increased — many workers had to <u>retrain</u> in jobs that would help the war effort. The plan was to make Germany <u>self-sufficient</u>, so it wasn't reliant on foreign goods.

The outbreak of War changed the Economy

1) More men were drafted into the <u>army</u> — which meant more <u>women</u> had to work, especially after <u>1941</u> when German forces were doing badly in <u>Russia</u>.
2) <u>Albert Speer</u> was appointed Minister of Armaments in 1942. From 1942 to 1944 weapons production tripled.
3) Later in the war, Germany used <u>slave labour</u> from conquered countries to help its war effort.
4) <u>Industries</u> which weren't related to the war effort were <u>neglected</u>.
5) German society <u>suffered</u> badly through the war with many civilians being <u>killed</u> through <u>Allied bombing raids</u>. It was soon harder to turn a blind eye to the bad side of Nazi policies.

Hitler reduced unemployment — and gained popularity...

Hitler provided new jobs and helped Germany recover from the <u>Depression</u> (see p.8).

Young People and Women

The Nazis believed that to control the future they had to influence children and their mothers.

The Nazis created powerful Youth Groups

1) Hitler knew that loyalty from young people was essential if the Nazis were to remain strong.
2) Boys aged fourteen upwards were recruited to the Hitler Youth, which was compulsory from 1939. Girls aged from fourteen joined the League of German Maidens.
3) Boys wore military-style uniforms, and took part in lots of physical exercise. Girls were mainly trained in domestic skills like sewing.
4) The boys were being prepared to be soldiers, the girls to be wives and mothers.

The Nazis took over Education

1) Schools started teaching Nazi propaganda. Jews were banned from teaching in schools and universities. Most teachers joined the Nazi Teachers' Association and were trained in Nazi methods. Children had to report teachers who did not use them.
2) Subjects like history and biology were rewritten to fit in with Nazi ideas. Children were taught to be anti-Semitic and that World War I was lost because of Jews and communists.

Women were expected to raise Large Families

1) Nazis didn't want women to have too much freedom. They believed women's role was to support their families at home. Women existed to provide children.
2) The League of German Maidens spread the Nazi idea that it was an honour to produce large families for Germany. Nazis gave awards to women for doing this.
3) At school, girls studied subjects like cookery. It was stressed that they should choose 'Aryan' husbands.
4) Women were banned from being lawyers in 1936 and the Nazis did their best to stop them following other professions. The shortage of workers after 1937 meant more women had to go back to work. Many Nazi men did not like this.

Eight Main Reasons for Hitler's Popularity

It's hard to imagine now, but the Nazis were genuinely popular with many Germans at the time.

1) He gave the Germans jobs after the struggles and unemployment of the 1920s.
2) The people were taught the Nazi way from an early age.
3) He made them proud internationally — Germans had felt humiliated for a long time.
4) People felt much better off as industry expanded.
5) Massive rallies every year gave the impression of a strong, prosperous nation.
6) The army supported his aim to make Germany strong again.
7) Businesses liked the prosperity and the way Hitler attacked the communists.
8) People were frightened to protest against Nazi methods — they knew they'd be arrested.

Hitler Youth — not like your local youth club, then...

Although the Nazis were destroyed in 1945, they expected to be in power a lot, lot longer. That's why they spent so much time and effort on the young — creating Nazis for the future.

Opposition to the Nazis

The Nazis had a tight grip on Germany, but some opposition remained.

Opposition was Weak under the Nazis

1) Most people who disagreed with the Nazis were afraid of the SS and the Gestapo. They were also afraid their friends and neighbours would inform on them if they criticised the regime.
2) Thousands of those who did voice opposition to the Nazis were sent to concentration camps.
3) Opposition within the party was crushed on the Night of the Long Knives (p.40).
4) Anti-Nazi activity had to be carried out in secret — which made it difficult for different groups to work together.
5) Nazi propaganda persuaded most people that they were better off under Hitler.

The Nazis Overcame most Resistance

1) Once in power, the Nazis banned communist groups and sent many communists to concentration camps.
2) Some opposition came from religious groups, especially after church land was confiscated.
3) Jehovah's Witnesses were persecuted for not supporting the regime, with many members sent to the concentration camps.
4) Some opponents of the Reich Church joined together as the Confessing Church. Hundreds of clergy were arrested, including Martin Niemöller, one of the Confessing Church's founders.
5) Catholic dissent was more widespread after 1937, when Pope Pius XI sent out a letter protesting at German nationalism and racism, which was read out in Catholic churches.
6) Catholic protesters had some success in reducing Nazi interference with the Church.

Not all Young People supported the Nazis

1) The Edelweiss Pirates were groups of rebellious young people who were difficult to control. They didn't like being told what to do, and used the slogan 'Everlasting war on Hitler Youth'.
2) Some Edelweiss Pirates even sided with the Allies during the war and several were executed.
3) Other groups, like the Swing Kids who liked banned jazz music, were more a nuisance than a serious threat.
4) In Munich in 1943, a group of students called the White Rose were arrested for using passive resistance methods like distributing anti-Nazi leaflets. Several, including Sophie and Hans Scholl, were executed.

Resistance in the Army grew during the War

1) As the war started to go badly, some believed Hitler was leading Germany to defeat.
2) There had been plots against Hitler from army officers before the war, but these became more serious after the German defeats at El Alamein and Stalingrad in 1942.
3) One of the most famous was a plot by Claus von Stauffenberg (and other German officers) to kill Hitler. He put a bomb in a meeting room, but Hitler survived and most of the plotters were executed in 1944.

It wasn't easy to stand against the Nazis...

In the end, it was losing the war which toppled the Nazis — not German resistance.

Persecution

The Holocaust was the persecution and mass murder of Jewish people by the Nazis.

Hitler believed Aryans were a Super-Race

1) The Nazis believed Aryans (whites) were the 'master race' and people of other ethnicities, like Jewish or Slavic people, were inferior.
2) The Nazis blamed Jewish people for problems in German society.
3) The Nazis wanted a German population of only 'pure' Aryan people who fitted their ideal. They wanted to eliminate people who were disabled, homosexual, held different beliefs, or weren't 'Aryan'.
4) Hitler was angry when an African-American called Jesse Owens took four gold medals at the 1936 Berlin Olympics, and when the German World Heavyweight Boxing Champion Max Schmeling was beaten by another African American, Joe Louis.

Persecution of the Jews Increased through the 1930s

In 1935 Hitler passed the Nuremberg Laws
1) These laws stopped Jews being German citizens.
2) They banned marriage between Jews and non-Jews in Germany.
3) They banned sexual relationships between Jews and non-Jews.

Kristallnacht 1938 — the Night of Broken Glass
1) A Jew murdered a German diplomat in Paris in November 1938.
2) There was rioting throughout Germany — thousands of Jewish shops were smashed, and thousands of Jews were arrested.

Jewish people were Moved to Ghettos

1) After the invasions of Poland and Russia more Jews came under Nazi control.
2) From 1940, Jewish people were forced to move into ghettos — separate districts of cities which were usually walled in and policed by armed guards. The largest was in Warsaw.
3) Conditions in the ghettos were terrible. Starvation and disease killed thousands. A rebellion in the Warsaw ghetto in 1943 was ruthlessly put down.
4) When Russia was invaded in 1941, soldiers followed with orders to kill every Jew they came across in the occupied towns and villages.

The Nazis began the Final Solution in 1942

1) The Final Solution was the Nazis' plan to destroy the Jewish people.
2) Death camps were built in Eastern Europe. Gas chambers were built for mass murder.
3) Mainly Jewish people were killed, but other groups were targeted as well, for example Slavs (Russians and Poles), Roma, black people, homosexuals, disabled people and communists.
4) Heinrich Himmler, head of the SS, was in overall charge of this 'final solution'.
5) Some death camps were: Auschwitz, Treblinka, Sobibor, Chelmno, Belzec.
6) By the end of the war, approximately 6 million Jewish people had been killed by the Nazis.

Nazi Germany — a climate of cruelty and fear...

The Jewish people suffered terribly at the hands of the Nazis — and you need to know how. This is horrific, and it's hard for us to understand how such cruelty could have been carried out. Remember — other groups were also persecuted including Roma (gypsies) and the disabled.

Revision Summary

Phew — it's question time again. Now's your chance to show off what you've learned — and to find out what you still need to practise. Germany between the wars is a tricky subject — make sure you know about the long-term consequences of the Versailles Treaty, and the reasons for the weakness of the Weimar government. Most difficult of all, you've got to be able to give clear arguments for why Hitler was able to come to power. Remember — it doesn't matter if you can't answer all the questions first time. Go over the section again and keep trying, until you can answer every one. And there's no point in cheating — that won't help you in the exams. So let's get going.

1) What was the name of the first President of the Weimar Republic? Which party did he belong to?

2) Why was the government based at Weimar?

3) What was the name of the parliament in the Weimar Republic?

4) Name the force which was started to keep the peace in Germany.

5) Give three reasons for discontent in Germany after World War I.

6) Where did the Spartacist Revolt and the Kapp Putsch take place?

7) Give the main results of the French occupation of the Ruhr in 1923.

8) Write a paragraph outlining the work of Gustav Stresemann.

9) Which party was responsible for the Munich Putsch? Who was its leader?

10) Name the paramilitary force which was set up to support the Nazis.

11) What was the title of the book Hitler wrote in prison?

12) Who beat Hitler in the Presidential elections of April 1932?

13) How did Hitler use the Reichstag Fire?

14) What did Hitler's Enabling Bill allow him to do in March 1933?

15) What was the Night of the Long Knives?

16) What title did Hitler give himself on the death of Hindenburg in 1934?

17) What were Gaue?

18) Which Nazi was put in charge of propaganda? Write about some of the methods he used.

19) What was the SS? What was the Gestapo?

20) Give an achievement of the Nazi programme of public works.

21) What was the 'Strength through Joy' programme? What organisation did workers have to join instead of trade unions?

22) Name the leading Nazi who was put in charge of the Luftwaffe.

23) In what ways did the Nazis make sure that young people followed their cause?

24) Which organisation did teachers in Nazi Germany have to join?

25) Give eight reasons why the German people followed the Nazis.

26) Give two reasons why opposition was weak under the Nazis.

27) What was the name of the church set up by Protestants who opposed the Reich Church?

28) Name the African-American athlete who won four gold medals at the Berlin Olympics in 1936.

29) What were the Nuremberg Laws? What did they do?

30) Describe what happened on the 'Night of Broken Glass'.

Russia Under the Tsars

Before the First World War, the Tsar held supreme power in Russia.

The Government of the Russian Empire was Unpopular

Tsar Nicholas II

Absolute ruler: His dynasty had ruled Russia for 300 years. Increasingly unpopular.

Peasants: 85% of people. Poor people using old, inefficient farming methods.

Industrial workers: Had low wages and poor working conditions. Industry was growing.

1) The Tsar was all-powerful — he ruled <u>without a parliament</u>, and most of the country's wealth and land was owned by a small noble class. The Church taught that the Tsar must be <u>obeyed</u>.

2) Peasant villages were controlled by the <u>mir</u> — a local council who interfered in everyone's business and had the power to <u>decide</u> whether a peasant was <u>allowed</u> to own or rent <u>land</u>.

3) The growth of <u>industry</u> meant there was a large working population in the towns — but conditions in the towns were <u>cramped</u> and the workers were <u>badly paid</u>.

4) In 1905 Russia was <u>defeated</u> in a war with Japan.

5) Poor conditions led to <u>strikes</u> and <u>demonstrations</u> — on 'Bloody Sunday' troops fired into a crowd of peaceful demonstrators in St Petersburg. There was <u>nearly</u> a popular <u>revolution</u>.

The Tsar allowed some Change and set up a Parliament

In <u>1905</u> Russia lost a war with Japan.

There were <u>food shortages</u>, <u>demonstrations</u> and <u>strikes</u>.

The <u>Duma</u> was set up. This was an elected assembly or <u>parliament</u>.

1) In the first <u>Duma</u> of 1906, the liberal <u>Constitutional Democratic Party</u> (known as the Cadets) won a majority. They demanded <u>control</u> of <u>taxes</u>, as the Tsar had promised them.

2) Instead he <u>dismissed</u> the Duma and many Liberals <u>fled</u> to Finland. New elections were held.

3) This time the Duma was even more radical — members of the <u>Marxist SDLP</u> (Social Democratic Labour Party — see p.49) <u>won</u> some seats from the Cadets. When the Tsar wanted to <u>arrest</u> several SDLP members as terrorists the Duma <u>refused</u> — so the Tsar <u>dismissed</u> it too.

4) The next two Dumas (1907-1914) <u>obeyed</u> the Tsar. The SDLP were not allowed to run as candidates and any known '<u>troublemakers</u>' were arrested and <u>imprisoned</u>.

5) The press was <u>censored</u> and a secret police was used to <u>spy</u> on people the Tsar feared.

6) The situation of the people hadn't improved and there was still a lot of <u>discontent</u> among the <u>poor</u> working classes.

Tsarist Russia — dumb and Duma...

The Tsar had <u>autocratic power</u> in 1914 — that means he had the final say on everything. But as events earlier in the century had shown, there were plenty of people who were prepared to go to great lengths pressing for <u>reform</u>.

Countdown to Revolution

Attempts were made to fix Russia's problems, but <u>World War I</u> made everything more difficult.

Attempted Reform hit Problems — 1906 to 1911

1) Prime Minister Stolypin wanted <u>economic reforms</u> — he was afraid that badly run industry could get out of control.

2) He <u>ended</u> the control of the <u>mir</u> over how land was distributed. Hard-working peasants could now rent or buy land to farm themselves — helped by special Peasant Banks. These better-off peasants were known as <u>kulaks</u>.

3) The <u>mir</u> system continued but became <u>less efficient</u> when the kulaks left — causing problems for the country's <u>food supply</u>.

4) Peasants in the mir farms <u>resented</u> the wealth of some kulaks.

5) Reform needed peace, but <u>Europe</u> was heading for <u>war</u>.

6) Stolypin was <u>murdered</u> in 1911 by a revolutionary.

Rasputin

Tsar Nicholas' wife was influenced by a 'Holy Man' called <u>Rasputin</u> who claimed supernatural powers to treat the Tsar's son for haemophilia — a disease where the blood won't clot. Rasputin became <u>powerful</u> and even sacked and appointed government ministers. He was <u>killed</u> by angry nobles in 1916 — but the Tsar's <u>authority</u> had been <u>undermined</u>.

The First World War caused more Problems

Patriotism and <u>loyalty</u> to the Tsar were <u>revived</u>. People wanted a short and victorious war, but:

1) There were <u>high casualties</u> — around 1 800 000 Russian soldiers dead by the end of 1917.

2) There was a <u>shortage</u> of rifles and equipment. Poor transport slowed supplies to the front.

3) Military <u>leadership</u> was <u>bad</u> — the Tsar took <u>personal command</u> in 1915. This also meant he was often <u>away</u> at the Eastern Front — leaving his <u>unpopular wife</u> in charge in the capital.

4) The Russian army was <u>pushed back</u> by the <u>Germans</u> and there was a stalemate (see p. 86).

5) <u>Inflation</u> meant that prices at home went up massively.

6) There was widespread hunger and <u>food and fuel shortages</u> at home.

The 'February' Revolution of 1917

1) Demonstrations and food <u>riots</u> suddenly broke out in the capital city of Petrograd.

2) The Tsar had <u>lost support</u> and control — when his <u>soldiers</u> were ordered to fire on the mobs many refused or <u>deserted</u> to join the rioting workers.

3) The Tsar <u>gave up</u> the throne. A Provisional Government was formed under the leadership of Prince Lvov until July, and then Kerensky. Russia was now a <u>republic</u>.

4) The main revolutionary parties were taken by surprise — this was a real <u>people's revolution</u> caused by sudden risings of <u>workers</u> and <u>soldiers</u> sick of the war, <u>shortages</u> and high <u>prices</u>.

5) This meant that the new government could face <u>opposition</u> from the revolutionaries, who wanted power for themselves — among them, a group from the SDLP called the <u>Bolsheviks</u>.

The end of Tsarism — the people were revolting...

The <u>Russian calendar</u> was behind the Western one — by about two weeks. This means the '<u>February</u>' <u>revolution</u> took place in our <u>March</u> (and the later 'October' revolution took place in our November) — which can be confusing. In 1918, they switched to the same system as ours.

The Bolsheviks

The Bolshevik Party wanted power in Russia — it held <u>Marxist</u> beliefs.

Marxism said Capitalism was Wrong

1) Capitalism is the economic system based on <u>business</u> — selling things to make a <u>profit</u>.
2) <u>Marx</u>, a 19th-century political thinker, said this was <u>unjust</u> because thousands of workers were receiving low wages for labour that made a tiny elite class very rich.
3) According to Marx, history is a process of <u>development</u> towards an ideal society — change comes because of <u>class struggle</u> between the middle class and working class.
4) This would in time lead to a <u>violent revolution</u> by the workers. After the revolution, the means of <u>production</u> would be used for everyone's benefit and <u>shared</u> — this is called <u>communism</u>.

The SDLP were the Marxist Party in Russia

In the late 1890s and early 1900s, the SDLP <u>encouraged</u> the industrial workers in the towns to <u>protest</u> against their terrible living conditions. They hoped to <u>create</u> a situation where a <u>Marxist revolution</u> could take place. Many of them were <u>exiled</u> by the Tsarist government — this was one reason they weren't involved in the February Revolution.

The Bolsheviks came out of the SDLP

Lenin

1) At the Social Democrat Conference of 1903, the SDLP <u>quarrelled</u> over whether to become a <u>mass party</u> (open to anyone) or to remain a <u>small party</u> of dedicated members working towards revolution.
2) The party <u>split</u> into <u>Bolsheviks</u> who wanted a small party and were led by <u>Lenin</u>, and <u>Mensheviks</u> led by <u>Martov</u> who wanted a mass party.

Vladimir Ilyich Lenin was the Bolshevik leader. He was a <u>clever thinker</u> and a <u>practical</u> man — he knew how to take advantage of events.

The Bolsheviks were a Small Party

1) At first, the Bolsheviks were <u>too small</u> a party to make much <u>impact</u> on the workers.
2) During the war, Lenin was in <u>exile</u> in Switzerland. When the February Revolution came he returned to Russia to rally the Bolshevik cause.
3) The Germans <u>helped</u> him to return in a sealed train in April 1917, because they <u>hoped</u> he would cause another <u>revolution</u> and that Russia would <u>end</u> the war.

Lenin's 'April Theses' Urged Revolution

1) Lenin issued a document called the <u>April Theses</u>, promising '<u>peace, bread, land and freedom</u>'.
2) He called for an <u>end</u> to the 'capitalist' war, and demanded that <u>power</u> should be given to the <u>Soviets</u> — elected committees of workers, peasants and soldiers which had started up in 1905 and had given <u>leadership</u> to the people during the February Revolution.
3) He demanded a revolution <u>against</u> the Provisional Government as soon as possible.

Peace + Land + Bread

Learn your theory — it's easy Marx...

Make sure you know <u>how</u> the Bolsheviks were formed and <u>what</u> they stood for. The <u>April Theses</u> are important too — <u>no one</u> expected Lenin to attack the Provisional Government.

50

The Provisional Government

The situation was <u>very tricky</u> for the Provisional Government.

The Provisional Government had Problems

1) It <u>wasn't</u> supposed to <u>stay</u> in power — but the economic crisis made <u>elections impossible</u>.
2) <u>Inflation</u> grew even <u>worse</u>. Prices were ten times higher than 1914 by November 1917.
3) Food shortages became worse and peasants began to <u>seize land</u> from noble estates.
4) The new government <u>didn't end</u> the war — soldiers and sailors began to <u>mutiny</u>.
5) A <u>network</u> of <u>Soviets</u> was established — the <u>Petrograd Soviet</u> became an alternative government. Key workers were told to strike to <u>undermine</u> the Provisional Government.
6) The Petrograd Soviet issued <u>'Order No. 1'</u> which said that soldiers shouldn't obey orders from the Provisional Government if they were opposed by the Soviet.

Provisional Government → inflation × 10 → food shortages → didn't end war → army and navy mutinies → network of soviets → ?

The Soviets demanded an <u>end</u> to the war, but the army <u>attacked</u> the German forces in June 1917. After early Russian success the Germans <u>counter-attacked</u>, forcing a <u>retreat</u> and the <u>collapse</u> of morale and discipline in the Russian army.

The Bolsheviks Prepared for Further Revolution

The Bolsheviks gained <u>increasing support</u> among workers and soldiers with their slogan:

1) In July 1917 the Bolsheviks tried to <u>take control</u> of the government but were <u>defeated</u> and <u>Lenin</u> was forced to leave the country and <u>flee</u> to Finland.

All power to the Soviets

Kerensky had turned public opinion against him by accusing him of being a German agent.
2) <u>Leon Trotsky</u> led the <u>Red Guards</u> — a Bolshevik military force. At the same time, the Bolsheviks won control of the Soviets, and Trotsky was <u>Chairman</u> of the Petrograd Soviet.
3) Peasants <u>attacked</u> kulaks and <u>took land</u> from the Church and nobles.
4) Many <u>soldiers</u> started to <u>desert</u> from the army and returned home.

General Kornilov Attempted a Military Coup

1) In September 1917, the Russian Commander in Chief, General <u>Kornilov</u>, turned his army back from the Front and <u>marched against</u> the Provisional Government determined to seize power.
2) Kerensky had to <u>give weapons</u> to the Bolsheviks and the Petrograd Soviet to <u>save</u> his government from a military takeover.
3) <u>Bolshevik</u> railway workers and <u>Red Guards</u> were waiting to stop Kornilov's advance — but all his soldiers <u>deserted</u> him and he fled.
4) The Bolsheviks were now the <u>real power</u> in Russia, and Lenin <u>encouraged</u> Trotsky to prepare plans for seizing power.

The Bolshevik Press — it was red all over...

The Provisional Government was only supposed to be <u>temporary</u>, which was one of the reasons it was so vulnerable to attempts to <u>overthrow</u> it. Make sure you learn all the <u>events</u> that eventually led to its <u>downfall</u> and remember that the Russian <u>calendar</u> was different to ours, too.

The Bolsheviks Seize Power

The 'October' Revolution of 1917

The <u>Bolshevik Central Committee</u> under Lenin <u>voted</u> for <u>revolution</u>. Detailed plans were made by Trotsky to seize important buildings in Petrograd and arrest Ministers. The revolution started on <u>24th October</u> and the Bolsheviks were in control by the next day.

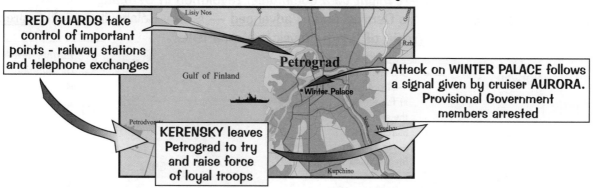

RED GUARDS take control of important points - railway stations and telephone exchanges

Attack on **WINTER PALACE** follows a signal given by cruiser **AURORA**. Provisional Government members arrested

KERENSKY leaves Petrograd to try and raise force of loyal troops

There were only 250 000 Bolsheviks in Russia, controlling a small part of the country — <u>civil war</u> was inevitable as there were <u>many</u> people who were <u>opposed</u> to Bolshevik rule.

Lenin was <u>ruthless</u> and <u>determined</u> to keep power. He knew a strong government was needed — so the ideals of communism had to wait.

The Bolsheviks Established Control

1) The <u>All-Russian Congress of Soviets</u> gave <u>power</u> to the <u>Soviet Council of People's Commissars</u> under Lenin, on 26th October 1917.
2) <u>Soldiers</u> were sent into the countryside to <u>seize grain</u> to feed the towns.
3) The Bolsheviks <u>controlled</u> the main centres of power and used <u>telegraph communications</u> to spread their revolutionary message to local groups.
4) <u>Elections</u> were held for a new constituent assembly. Bolsheviks won 168 seats out of 703, with <u>most seats</u> going to the <u>Socialist Revolutionary Party</u> (SRP), who had peasant support.
5) After one day the Red Guards <u>closed down</u> the Assembly — January 1918.
6) The Bolsheviks became the <u>Communist Party</u>, the only legal party in Russia.
7) Lenin made two decrees (orders) — the <u>Decree on Land</u> nationalised all land in Russia and the <u>Decree on Peace</u> called for peace with Germany.

The Reasons for the Bolshevik Success

1) They were <u>strong</u> in key political and administrative centres — especially <u>Petrograd</u>.
2) They had their <u>own</u> trained <u>military force</u> — the Red Guards.
3) They were ruthless and <u>planned clear strategies</u> — they were prepared for swift action.
4) They were <u>practical</u> — they recognised that the time for a true Marxist revolution was a long way off and so they <u>changed</u> their policies in order to seize power at the first chance. They claimed they ran a <u>socialist government</u> which was trying to create the <u>right conditions</u> for communism in the <u>long term</u> — so in the <u>short term</u> they could do <u>whatever</u> they liked.
5) The continuing problems of war and famine, and the breakdown of law and order, <u>weren't</u> dealt with by the Provisional Government, who had become a <u>weak target</u>.
6) The vision and ability of <u>Lenin</u> — he was a <u>quick-thinking</u> leader who inspired his party.

"Learn it all well" — Lenin's Decree on Revision...

The <u>October Revolution</u> (a.k.a. the 'November' Revolution due to Russia's calendar issues) was one of those big moments in history when a relatively <u>small group of people</u> have a <u>huge impact</u>.

1918 — Ending the German War

The Bolsheviks took Russia out of one war, and prepared for another one.

The Germans were Advancing

1) The Bolsheviks signed an armistice with the Germans, hoping to delay the peace treaties because they thought there might be a communist revolution in Germany too.

2) This didn't happen, and the German armies advanced — so the Bolsheviks quickly agreed to the harsh terms of the Treaty of Brest-Litovsk in March 1918.

Germany was defeated by the Western Allies later in 1918 and some lands were regained.

A Civil War was Inevitable

Lenin and Trotsky were prepared for this. The reasons the civil war broke out were:

1) The communists had seized power suddenly and repressed the elected Constituent Assembly — they had also outlawed political opposition, so many people saw them as a danger.

2) Anti-communist army officers were no longer fighting Germany — many were royalists and wanted the return of the Tsar — and now they could attack the communists.

3) Communism wanted a world revolution — the Comintern (the Communist International) was formed under Zinoviev to promote revolution abroad and to encourage friendly governments in nearby European countries.

> The government moved from Petrograd to Moscow in 1918 — Leon Trotsky began to build an efficient Red Army to fight the civil war.

The civil war — not a very polite affair...

Remember — a civil war was the last thing Russia needed after the disasters of the First World War, but the communists knew it was coming, which was why they made peace with Germany at any cost. Scribble down the names of the lands lost by Russia.

The Civil War 1918-1921

The first big challenge for the new Bolshevik government was the brutal civil war.

Anti-Communist forces surrounded Red Russia

1) These armies were called the 'Whites' — the colour of the Tsarist state.
2) There were many White groups who often had different aims and purposes — a key problem.
3) Britain, France and the USA sent troops to help the Whites — trying to restart a war on Germany's Eastern Front, and worried by communist ideas of world revolution.

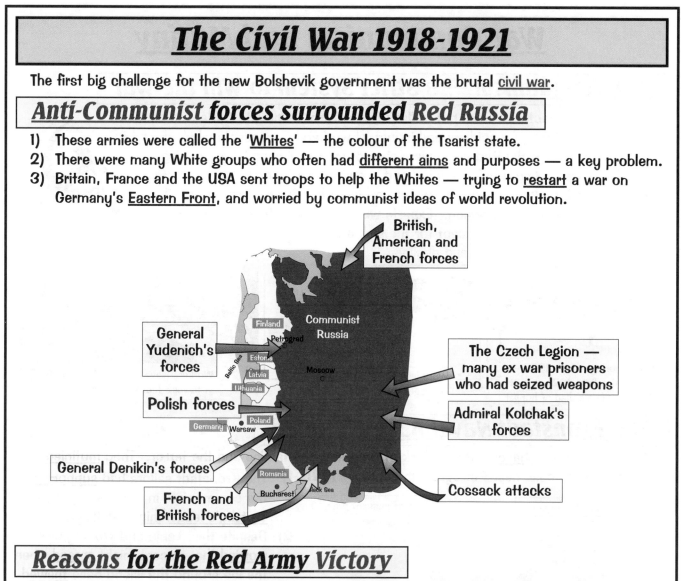

Reasons for the Red Army Victory

1) Red forces were united, while White forces were divided and didn't work together to surround their enemy — this meant the Reds could fight the White armies one by one, instead of fighting on several fronts at the same time. Trotsky was also a brilliant leader.
2) White forces were a long way apart and couldn't stay in touch to coordinate attacks. Some had different political opinions — which meant they didn't want to work together.
3) Patriotic Russians supported the Reds — the Whites were led by nobles and foreign armies.
4) Foreign military support was soon withdrawn as it became clear the Reds would win.
5) The communists controlled the main cities and communications systems — and the railways.
6) The strict and ruthless laws of War Communism helped obtain supplies for the Reds.
7) When the Red Army had defeated its enemies in Russia it carried on and pushed into Poland, hoping to link up with communists in Germany to spread revolution throughout Europe — but it was defeated by the Poles outside Warsaw in late 1920. The war ended with a treaty in 1921.

The Tsar and his Family were Killed

1) The Tsar and his family were held prisoner in a house at Ekaterinburg, because the communists knew they were an important symbol for the White cause.
2) They were executed by the Bolsheviks in 1918 as White forces approached the town.

Success in Europe — the Reds go marching on...

Plenty for you to learn here — looking at the map you'd have thought the Whites would win easily. Focus on the Whites' lack of coordination and the strength of communist control.

War Communism and Mutiny

War Communism — a Strict System to Win the War

1) Farms and factories were put under <u>state</u> control — private trade was banned.
2) <u>Food was taken</u> for soldiers and industrial workers — peasants who <u>refused</u> to hand it over to the Red Army were shot or sent to forced <u>labour camps</u>.
3) The <u>secret police</u> (Cheka) hunted and executed any <u>enemies</u> of the state.
4) Industrial workers <u>weren't allowed</u> to <u>strike</u> or be absent from work. They could be sent to any region. Experts were brought in to improve efficiency.
5) <u>All adults</u> had to <u>work</u> except for the sick and pregnant women.
6) The results were <u>famine</u> and <u>decline</u>.

Food shortages from 1920 — and famine from 1921 — over 7 million people died of hunger

Worthless currency abandoned — wages paid in fuel and food

Workers leave cities, little food in towns. Industry declines

The Kronstadt Naval Base Mutinied

The sailors were <u>unhappy</u> with the lack of progress, the famine and the terror. They <u>mutinied</u> and seized the base near Petrograd, in February 1921.

Free speech and press

Sale of peasant grain

Ballot Box

Kronstadt rebels demands

Free elections for Soviets

Free trade unions

1) The Kronstadt sailors had <u>supported</u> the communists in 1917 — especially <u>Trotsky's leadership</u> in Petrograd.
2) Despite this, Lenin and Trotsky were <u>worried</u> that dissent might <u>spread</u> when the ice around the island base <u>thawed</u> and let the sailors leave.
3) Trotsky <u>ordered</u> the Red Army to <u>put down</u> the mutiny.
4) The Red Army <u>attacked</u>, losing many men, but <u>captured</u> it in a brutal battle.
5) Many rebels were <u>killed</u> in the fighting — those who were left were either <u>executed</u> or <u>imprisoned</u> as traitors.

There were other revolts — peasants in Tambov Province <u>robbed</u> food convoys and many factories suffered <u>strikes</u> and <u>unrest</u>.

Lenin Decided to Change Communist Policy

1) Communism was pushing ahead <u>'too fast'</u> — Trotsky had recognised the economic crisis in 1920 and suggested a <u>change of policy</u> to encourage businesses. Lenin <u>rejected</u> this at first.
2) Now the civil war was won, the communists needed to <u>keep control</u> of public opinion.
3) This meant a policy of <u>complete party unity</u> — no dissent or splits allowed.
4) In 1921 Lenin introduced the <u>New Economic Policy (NEP)</u> to restore <u>order</u> and increase <u>prosperity</u> after the chaos of revolution, civil war and War Communism.

War Communism — not an overwhelming success then...

The Bolsheviks survived in part due to Lenin's willingness to change a <u>failing policy</u>.

The New Economic Policy

The New Economic Policy Reversed War Communism

1) Peasants could <u>sell</u> surplus food produce and pay <u>tax</u> on profits.
2) <u>Small businesses</u>, like shops and small factories, no longer <u>had</u> to be state-owned — they could therefore make a profit.
3) Vital <u>industries</u> such as coal, iron, steel, railways, shipping and finance stayed in state hands. But here experts were brought in on <u>higher salaries</u>, and extra wages were paid for <u>efficiency</u>.

> The <u>NEP</u> allowed <u>economic recovery</u> — by 1928 industrial and food production levels were about the same as in 1914, and some people grew rich.

Communist political Control Grew

1) A 'purge' in 1921 <u>expelled</u> about a third of Party members — those who <u>didn't agree</u> with Lenin.
2) Communist governments were <u>imposed</u> in areas <u>recaptured</u> in the civil war, against the will of independent nationalists such as in the <u>Ukraine</u>.
3) A <u>new constitution</u> established the <u>USSR</u> — Union of Soviet Socialist Republics.
4) Each Republic had a government with some policy freedom, but they all <u>had</u> to be communist, and the system was run centrally by the <u>Politburo</u> — the senior council.

Lenin Died on Jan 21, 1924

1870	Lenin born.
1898	First Congress of the SDLP.
1903	Bolsheviks (majority) split from Mensheviks (minority).
1917	February — First Revolution — Provisional Government (Kerensky).
	April — Lenin outlines plans to overthrow government.
	July — Bolshevik rising defeated.
	October — Bolshevik communist revolution and takeover.
1918	March — Peace treaty with Germany (Brest-Litovsk)
1918-21	Civil war. Reds vs Whites.
1921	Famine. Kronstadt rebellion. New Economic Policy.
1922	Lenin ill after a stroke. Policy led by Stalin, Zinoviev and Kamenev.

Lenin died in 1924. Petrograd was renamed <u>Leningrad</u> in his honour.

Lenin's Key Strengths as a Leader

1) His <u>organisation</u> and <u>leadership</u> of the Bolshevik party transformed it.
2) He had a <u>pragmatic</u> and <u>realistic</u> approach to problems.
3) He was able to '<u>seize the moment</u>', which was vital in the Bolsheviks gaining power.
4) He could be <u>ruthless</u> — he set up the Cheka (secret police) and the labour camps. He also wasn't afraid to use force to put down the Kronstadt mutiny.
5) He was able to <u>change</u> his <u>policies</u> — e.g. he was able to adopt War Communism to win the civil war, and then to introduce the NEP afterwards to help the economy recover.

The New Economic Policy — so new it wasn't even communist...

The NEP <u>reversed</u> War Communism. The easiest way to get them learned is to <u>compare</u> the two. Scribble a list of the <u>main details</u> of each policy — especially the differences between them.

The Struggle for Power

Lenin's death meant that there was a <u>vacancy</u> at the top of the Party.

Several Leaders Struggled to Succeed Lenin

1) <u>TROTSKY</u> was the most able, and <u>popular</u> with the <u>army</u> and <u>Party members</u>. He led the Red Army brilliantly during the civil war, but some people thought he was too <u>arrogant</u> and he lacked support in the Politburo. He had been a <u>Menshevik</u> and he often made enemies.
2) <u>ZINOVIEV</u> and <u>KAMENEV</u> were left-wingers who agreed with Trotsky's ideas about <u>state control</u> of land and continuing the <u>revolution</u>. But they were determined to <u>stop Trotsky</u> becoming Party leader. Zinoviev was a popular man and had been a friend of Lenin.
3) <u>STALIN</u> didn't seem likely to lead the party. He had accumulated power through <u>good organisation</u> 'behind the scenes' in his work as <u>General Secretary</u> of the Party.

Lenin's testament talked about who might succeed him — he said <u>Trotsky</u> was <u>arrogant</u> but <u>able</u> and said <u>Stalin</u> should be <u>removed from office</u> because he was <u>too rude</u> and <u>ambitious</u>.

Trotsky and Stalin Had a War of Ideas

Leon Trotsky

...wanted <u>revolution</u> to <u>spread</u> to other countries — he called for the USSR to work for a world revolution.

Joseph Stalin

...and most of the Party wanted a period of <u>peace</u> and <u>rebuilding</u> in the USSR — 'Communism in one country'.

How Stalin Made Himself All-Powerful

1) Stalin controlled the Communist Party — he <u>appointed</u> people <u>loyal</u> to him to senior positions.
2) This meant Stalin's <u>rivals</u> had <u>no support</u> in the Party, and he <u>suppressed</u> Lenin's testament.
3) Only <u>Party members</u> could hold <u>government positions</u> and they were <u>chosen</u> by Party <u>voting</u>. It was a <u>one-party state</u>.
4) By the late 1920s Stalin had enough Party support to have his <u>rivals voted out</u> of power.

Stalin Destroyed the Leftists and the Rightists

1) Stalin <u>joined</u> Zinoviev and Kamenev <u>against</u> Trotsky — who was dismissed as Commissar for War in 1925. '<u>Socialism in one country</u>' became Party policy in 1925.
2) Trotsky was isolated — and <u>thrown out</u> of the Communist Party in 1927.
3) <u>New</u> members were elected to the Politburo, <u>loyal</u> to Stalin. At this time Stalin <u>supported the NEP</u> and gradual reform of the economy. The '<u>leftist</u>' Zinoviev and Kamenev were <u>dismissed</u> from the Politburo because they believed in <u>fast economic modernisation</u> (one of Trotsky's main ideas). They joined Trotsky to protest against Stalin and were expelled from the Party.
4) Trotsky was <u>exiled</u> to Kazakhstan in 1928, and forced to <u>leave</u> the USSR in 1929.
5) But in 1928 Stalin adopted <u>fast modernisation</u> instead of the NEP. This swing to the left meant he could now <u>remove</u> the leading figures on the <u>right</u> of the party, such as Bukharin and Rykov who supported the NEP, and could have been a threat to his position.
6) By 1929 he was in <u>complete control</u> as leader of the Communist Party and the USSR.

Stalin was a spin doctor — he changed the revolution...

The key factor in Stalin's rise was <u>Party control</u>. Remember, the Party <u>wasn't</u> the same as the government. But the USSR's constitution could be <u>abused</u> by anyone controlling the Party.

The Terror and the Purges

Stalin was single-minded on his way to the top — and terrifying when he got there.

Stalin was Ruthless in Destroying Rivals

GEORGIA
Russia
Black Sea
Tbilisi
Turkey
Armenia
Azerbaijan
Yerevan
Stepankert
Iran

1) Born in 1879 in the Republic of Georgia, his real name was Joseph Jughashvili. He had studied to become a priest, but became a Bolshevik. He changed his name to Stalin ('man of steel') when he was imprisoned as a revolutionary.

2) He was an organiser who began by making speeches, and organising strikes and bank raids to aid Bolshevik funds. He was efficient at routine organisation which many thought was dull.

3) His power base came from being General Secretary of the Party after 1922 — by controlling Party appointments he could control who was given government roles, and chose people loyal to him.

4) By 1930 he was undisputed leader of Russia, but he became terrified that others wanted to overthrow him — this made him determined to get rid of rivals.

The Kirov Murder Began a Purge

1) Kirov was the popular head of the Party in Leningrad — he was murdered in 1934.

2) Some historians think Stalin was responsible for his death — in 1956 Stalin's successor, Khrushchev, blamed Stalin for the murder, but there is no clear proof.

3) Immediately Stalin ordered a purge of people he believed were involved in a conspiracy against Kirov and against himself — but Kirov's murderer was never put on trial.

4) In 1935-6, many 'old' communists like Zinoviev and Kamenev were arrested and charged in 'show trials'. They were forced by torture or threats to confess to betraying Stalin.

5) No one knows exactly what was true and what was invented by Stalin's torturers.

6) One claim was that the exiled Trotsky was plotting with senior leaders to take power.

Soon the Purges Reached Ordinary People

1) Stalin used terror to prevent disloyalty — anyone suspected of being disloyal to Stalin was taken away by the NKVD (the new secret police).

2) Most were shot or sent to labour camps.

3) People who wanted to avoid arrest did so by providing information about others — even if it was false.

4) Stalin's wife killed herself (or was murdered) after a purge at the university where she was a teacher.

5) The exiled Trotsky condemned Stalin's purges from his home in Mexico, calling for a new revolution. In 1940 he was murdered by one of Stalin's agents.

6) The total number of people killed by Stalin's regime is uncertain — but some estimates are as high as ten million.

Party	1/3 purged
Congress delegates	1/2 purged
Generals & Admirals	4/5 purged
Old Communists Politburo	7/8 purged

The purges — a vicious circle...

Confusing stuff — but you need to get it straight. Under torture people invented all sorts of things to try to save themselves. Stalin started to believe there really was a plot against him.

Stalin the Dictator

Stalin <u>tightened</u> his brutal grip on the USSR.

Stalin Controlled all Information

1) Artists and writers had to <u>follow</u> the <u>Party line</u>, creating 'useful' art for the workers.
2) Newspapers, cinema and radio spread <u>propaganda</u> about the <u>heroic workers' struggle</u> and created a <u>cult of personality</u> which made Stalin look like a great and heroic leader. Criticism was <u>banned</u>.
3) <u>History</u> was <u>rewritten</u> so that Stalin became more <u>important</u> in the story of the October Revolution than he really had been at the time.
4) <u>Trotsky</u> became a '<u>non-person</u>' — his name was removed from history books and articles, and his picture was rubbed out of old photos as though he had never existed.
5) <u>Photographs</u> were <u>altered</u> to show Stalin as a close friend and ally of Lenin.

> <u>Top Tip</u>: source material in the exams could be <u>propaganda</u> — opinion and not just fact. To get top marks you've got to say which points are true and which aren't, and explain what <u>opinion</u> the source expresses.

The Purges Weakened the USSR

The terror slowed down by the end of the 1930s, but it had <u>serious consequences</u>:
1) Many of the most gifted and able citizens had <u>disappeared</u> — killed or sent to camps.
2) The <u>army</u> and <u>navy</u> was seriously <u>weakened</u> by the loss of most senior officers.
3) Industrial and technical <u>progress</u> was <u>hampered</u> by the loss of top scientists and engineers.
4) In 1936 a <u>new constitution</u> was brought in — every four years there were to be elections and only official Party candidates were allowed to stand. Power was kept in the Politburo.

The Communists Attacked the Church

1) The Russian Orthodox Church had been a powerful <u>supporter</u> of the <u>Tsar</u>.
2) The communist <u>government</u> began to <u>take</u> Church property and land — these were valuable assets for the Party. Christians were persecuted as a political threat to communism and priests were <u>murdered</u> or <u>exiled</u>.
3) In 1929 the Church was <u>banned</u> from any activity except leading worship.
4) By 1939 a <u>few hundred</u> churches <u>remained active</u> — the state claimed the promise of freedom of conscience in the 1936 constitution was being honoured.
5) <u>Many</u> people were <u>still believers</u> — nearly half the population in 1940.

Stalin's Russia was a Dictatorship

1) Stalin <u>ran everything</u> — his policies were often completely different from communist ideas.
2) Party '<u>apparatchiks</u>' — members loyal to Stalin — received <u>privileges</u> like holidays, flats etc.
3) Most people lived in <u>fear</u> but were <u>unable</u> to speak out.

Stalin got stronger — the USSR suffered...

Sources often mix facts with opinions. Your job is to <u>separate</u> the two, and find out why a source gives a particular <u>opinion</u>, and why it may <u>ignore</u> some of the facts. Think about <u>who</u> wrote it, <u>why</u> they wrote it, and <u>when</u> they wrote it — and how much they <u>really</u> knew.

The Five-Year Plans

The Party used targets to <u>increase the pace</u> of industrialisation.

The USSR still had a <u>Poor Economy</u>

1) The NEP had made some progress, but more rapid <u>growth</u> was <u>needed</u> for the USSR to <u>catch up</u> with the industrialised West and their economies.
2) Stalin adopted Trotsky's ideas for a programme of <u>fast state-controlled modernisation</u> to speed up production. Lenin's policy of the NEP was dropped.
3) The state took over planning for industry and agriculture with a commission called <u>Gosplan</u> to set targets for achievement.

The <u>First Five-Year Plan</u> was started in 1928

1) A <u>Five-Year Plan</u> set <u>targets</u> for all basic industrial factories and workers.
2) The plan concentrated on basic <u>heavy industry</u> — coal, steel, railways, electricity, machinery.
3) Actual <u>production</u> figures were <u>lower</u> than the targets, but remarkable <u>growth</u> in <u>output</u> was achieved.

In 1933 a Second Five-Year Plan was <u>Started</u>

1) Some parts of the second plan were achieved, but <u>fear</u> at the rise of Adolf Hitler in Nazi Germany meant more <u>development</u> took place in the <u>armaments</u> industry than any other.
2) A <u>third</u> Five-Year Plan started in 1938, but was even more <u>disrupted</u> by war preparation and the German invasion of 1941.

> In under 10 years, the USSR had almost <u>doubled</u> its industrial output — the price was <u>misery</u> and <u>low living standards</u> for Soviet workers.

There were <u>Serious Problems with the Plans</u>

1) <u>New towns</u>, <u>cities</u> and <u>industrial zones</u> were set up — often with <u>poor quality</u> housing.
2) <u>Long hours</u> were worked for <u>low pay</u>, and higher wages were offered to foreign workers with special skills required to work on new schemes.
3) <u>Bonuses</u> were given for workers who could improve upon production targets as an inspiration to others — e.g. Alexei <u>Stakhanov</u>, whose coal mining team dramatically increased its output — but these were often <u>unrealistic targets</u> for most workers.
4) Much of the work was done by forced <u>labour camps</u> of criminals and political prisoners.
5) The targets were <u>propaganda</u> tools — the government said they'd been broken but often it's hard to tell how much was really achieved and how much was just propaganda.

Five years — I've got a cunning plan...

Communist Party propaganda used Stakhanov as an image of a <u>heroic worker</u> in the press and news reels. A <u>'Stakhanovite' movement</u> began which encouraged workers to match this ideal.

Collectivisation

Communism was <u>forced</u> on the countryside.

Food Production *had to be* Increased

1) It was vital to <u>increase</u> the <u>food supplies</u> to workers in the towns and cities or the five-year plans <u>wouldn't</u> succeed.
2) Millions of peasants <u>hid</u> food away and <u>didn't support</u> the communists.
3) They were often <u>poor</u> and had no time-saving equipment.
4) Many richer peasants, or <u>kulaks</u> (see p.48), were <u>influential</u> in the villages, which annoyed the local Communist Party secretaries.

In 1929 Stalin began Collectivising All Farms

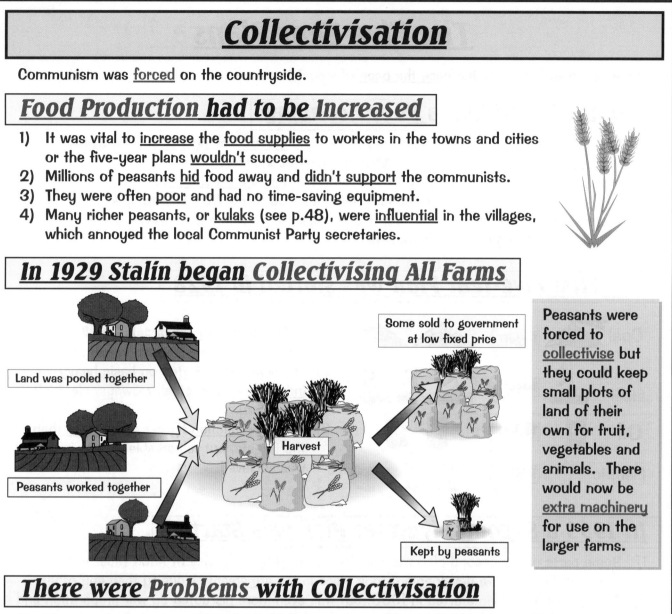

Land was pooled together

Peasants worked together

Harvest

Some sold to government at low fixed price

Kept by peasants

Peasants were forced to <u>collectivise</u> but they could keep small plots of land of their own for fruit, vegetables and animals. There would now be <u>extra machinery</u> for use on the larger farms.

There were Problems with Collectivisation

1) The <u>speed</u> of change required would <u>destroy</u> the <u>traditional</u> peasant way of life.
2) The peasants <u>resisted</u> this change and didn't want to give up land — especially the kulaks.
3) The collectives were forced to grow <u>particular crops</u> needed for industry, export or food for workers and they had to supply a <u>specific amount</u> to the state, whether the harvest was good or bad. <u>Party officials</u> were brought in to run collectives — this was <u>resented</u>.

Stalin Declared War *on the* Kulaks

1) Some of the peasants <u>refused</u> to collectivise, and Stalin <u>blamed</u> the <u>kulaks</u>.
2) Stalin sent troops to <u>attack</u> what he called these 'enemies of the people'.
3) An estimated 3 million kulaks were killed. Some were <u>shot</u>. Others died from <u>starvation</u> or cold either on the way to <u>labour camps</u> or during their time working there.
4) Some villages were <u>surrounded</u> and <u>destroyed</u> — many kulaks <u>burned</u> their own crops and <u>killed</u> livestock in protest. This contributed to a <u>famine</u> in the Ukraine — around 5 million people died.
5) 1930 saw famine and a poor harvest, and <u>collectivisation</u> was <u>halted</u> briefly.

Putting the farms together — a collective disaster...

This is all pretty vicious I'm afraid — and it's going to get worse. <u>Collectivisation</u> is a really important topic — it was intended to <u>help</u> the five-year plans but the effects were horrific. Don't forget to learn the <u>main problems</u> with collectivisation. And remember that when things went wrong Stalin looked for someone to blame — the <u>kulaks</u> were scapegoats here.

The Results of Collectivisation

Collectivisation brought agriculture under <u>communist control</u> — but at a cost.

The Famine Continued into 1932-33

1) Millions were <u>dead</u> or <u>deported</u>.
2) <u>Grain</u> production was down and <u>animal</u> numbers had fallen.

After 1931 Collectivisation Began Again

1) By 1939 it was almost complete — <u>99%</u> of farming land had been <u>collectivised</u>.
2) The <u>kulaks</u> had been <u>eliminated</u> and the peasants left were afraid of communist power.
3) The <u>Communist Party</u> held absolute <u>authority</u> throughout rural Russia as it did in the cities.

There were Different Views of Collectivisation

In exam questions you may be presented with <u>different interpretations</u> of this issue.
Remember these are often <u>opinions</u>, mixing facts and ideas, and not always telling the truth:

The Positive View

1) It ended the forced <u>exploitation</u> of peasants by greedy landlords and got rid of the <u>greedy</u> and <u>troublesome</u> kulaks.
2) It helped peasants <u>work together</u>.
3) It provided <u>large-scale organisation</u> of food production for the farms.
4) This was <u>communism in practice</u>.
5) Soviet propaganda showed collective farms as a <u>triumph</u> for the state, and created a <u>myth</u> of the <u>happy worker</u>.

The Negative View

1) The changes were enforced by the <u>army</u> and by <u>law</u> — there was <u>no choice</u>.
2) The kulaks were <u>scapegoats</u> for inefficient food production in the past.
3) The policy led to the <u>murder</u> and <u>imprisonment</u> of millions of people.
4) The new system <u>didn't work</u> at first and a <u>bad harvest</u> combined with kulaks destroying crops and animals caused a <u>serious famine</u> — killing more people.

Propaganda and scapegoats — Stalin's key tactics...

Another important page for you to learn here — two views of collectivisation. Remember that neither side is giving pure facts — they're mixing them with opinions. It'll be up to you to tell <u>opinions</u> and <u>facts</u> apart in the exam, and use them to give a <u>balanced answer</u> to the question.

Life in the Soviet Union

Everyday life was <u>difficult</u> for many citizens of the USSR, but some did <u>better</u> than others.

Conditions were Harsh for millions of people

1) <u>Life was hard</u>, but it was <u>dangerous</u> to grumble — people feared being taken away by the secret police. Millions were shot or taken to labour camps during the purges (p.57).
2) Life in the <u>cities</u> was tough. <u>Discipline</u> was strict in the factories, and wages were low.
3) However, as a result of the rapid <u>industrialisation</u> there was almost <u>no unemployment</u>.
4) Life was probably worse for those in the countryside as a result of the <u>forced collectivisation</u>. Most people lived in <u>rural areas</u>, and in general they were far poorer than those in the cities. Only about a <u>quarter of Party members</u> were of <u>peasant origin</u>.

Some groups were "More Equal" than others

<u>Communism</u> was supposed to be about <u>equality</u>, but some people were better off than others.

1) <u>What people could buy</u> depended on a <u>system</u> based on <u>social grouping</u> — farmers, factory workers, engineers and Party managers had different places in the hierarchy. Those high up in the Party got the best goods and services. This also decided the standard of <u>medical treatment</u> people received.
2) <u>Social mobility</u> did increase as a result of the <u>technical colleges</u> which were opened during the first <u>Five-Year Plan</u>. Thousands of workers achieved <u>promotion</u> through <u>education</u>.

There were mixed fortunes for the Ethnic Minorities

1) Early Bolshevik ideology <u>supported</u> the rights of ethnic minorities, but the USSR <u>didn't grant</u> any real political <u>independence</u> to its non-Russian republics.
2) Some minorities suffered forcible <u>population transfers</u>. Stalin ordered <u>mass deportations</u> of ethnic Poles during the <u>1930s</u> and of people from the Baltic states after 1940. Many were sent north-east to Siberia.
3) The USSR followed a policy of 'decossackisation'. The Cossacks — a <u>military people</u> who had mostly fought against the Bolsheviks during the civil war (see p.53) — were forced from their traditional homeland.
4) Although communism was against <u>anti-Semitism</u>, <u>Stalin distrusted Jews</u> — partly because his enemy <u>Trotsky</u> was Jewish. Many <u>victims of the purges</u> were Jewish.

Women were supposed to be Equal

1) The revolution gave women <u>legal equality</u>. <u>Divorce</u> was simplified. The state provided many <u>communal creches</u>, <u>kitchens</u> and <u>laundries</u>, to help women to work outside the home on an equal basis with men.
2) During <u>1919-30</u> the Women's Department of the Communist Party — the <u>Zhenotdel</u> — organised political <u>training conferences</u> attended by <u>millions</u> of women. But there were always far fewer women than men in the Party.
3) In the 1930s Stalin introduced legislation to <u>restrict divorce</u> and reduce women's independence. The emphasis was increasingly on <u>stability and discipline</u>, rather than on equality. Women were expected to go out and work, while still fulfilling traditional roles when they got home.

Not an easy time to be Russian — or Ukrainian, Georgian...

Communist rule didn't affect everybody in the same way. Although it was terrible for many millions of people, for others there were <u>opportunities</u> they'd never have had under the Tsar.

Revision Summary

And now it's time for your favourite part of every section — those sublime revision questions. I bet you can't wait — but remember that this is a really big topic. Make sure you know the order of events and the names of all the key people in this section.

1) What was the name of the last Tsar?

2) What was the Duma?

3) Who was Rasputin?

4) Explain the impact that the First World War had on Russia.

5) Why was Kerensky's government 'Provisional' — and what does this mean?

6) What were the main beliefs of Marxism?

7) Why were communists split into Bolsheviks and Mensheviks?

8) What did the 'April Theses' promise?

9) Give three problems the Provisional Government faced.

10) Which General marched against the Provisional Government in September 1917?

11) How did the Bolsheviks seize power in 1917?

12) Give four reasons for the Bolsheviks' success?

13) Why were the Bolsheviks prepared to agree to the Brest-Litovsk Treaty?

14) Consider the events of the civil war — why did the 'Reds' win and the 'Whites' lose?

15) What were the results of the civil war on the economy, farming and industry?

16) What was the Kronstadt rebellion and how was it dealt with?

17) Write down the main features of the New Economic Policy, and its results.

18) When did Lenin die?

19) Write a short summary of Lenin's achievements.

20) What was the main difference in ideas between Stalin and Trotsky?

21) Why was Joseph Stalin able to win the struggle for power?

22) What were the purges?

23) What was the NKVD?

24) How was the Church changed by Stalin's rule?

25) Explain or make a diagram to show the targets of the first Five-Year Plan.

26) Make summary notes/diagrams to explain how a collective farm worked.

27) Why were many peasants opposed to a collective farm system?

28) Why did Stalin want to get rid of the 'kulaks' in the countryside?

29) Why was the early 1930s a time of famine?

30) Why were people afraid of complaining about working conditions in Stalin's Russia?

31) Which element of the first Five-Year Plan helped increase social mobility?

32) What was the name for the policy the USSR brought against the Cossacks?

Growth of Isolationism

America just wanted to be <u>alone</u>.

The USA Entered Late and Gained From World War One

1) The American economy <u>boomed</u> as a result of the First World War.
2) The USA exported <u>weapons</u> and <u>food</u> to Europe during the war.
3) The USA <u>joined</u> the Allied side in <u>1917</u> — but no fighting happened on American soil.
4) After the war, European countries whose industries had been damaged <u>bought American goods</u> with the help of <u>American loans</u>.

Cheap European Imports were seen as a Threat

1) American <u>businesses</u> were afraid that the USA would be flooded with <u>cheap European imports</u>.
2) <u>Unemployment</u> was higher in <u>Europe</u> so European workers were willing to work for <u>lower wages</u>. Businessmen were worried American consumers would start <u>buying European products</u> rather than the <u>more expensive</u> American ones.
   This would mean: • The <u>loss</u> of American <u>jobs</u>.
   • <u>Lower profits</u> for US companies.
   • Less money in <u>taxes</u> for the US government.

Warren G Harding raised tariffs to protect US Industry

President Harding

1) Harding was elected President in 1921. He brought in the <u>Emergency Tariff Act</u> of <u>May 1921</u>. A tariff is a <u>tax</u> on imported and exported goods. The act <u>increased</u> the tariff rates on <u>imported farm products</u>.
2) In 1922, the <u>Fordney-McCumber Tariff</u> gave the President the power to raise and lower the tariff rates.
3) Harding used the Fordney-McCumber Tariff to <u>raise duties</u> on both <u>factory</u> and <u>farm</u> goods.
4) He hoped to <u>protect</u> America from "<u>unfair</u>" European competition.

Immigration Control was increased

Before the First World War, America had followed an '<u>Open Doors</u>' policy that allowed almost <u>anybody</u> to move to the USA. But some Americans started <u>demanding</u> that this '<u>door</u>' be <u>closed</u>. The most <u>powerful</u> and <u>wealthy</u> cultural group in America at this time were people with mainly British ancestors — later known as the <u>White Anglo-Saxon Protestants</u> (WASPs).

1) Many WASPs believed that people such as <u>anarchists</u> and <u>communists</u> were coming into the USA and <u>undermining</u> the American way of life.
2) They were also alarmed at the number of <u>Asian</u>, <u>Catholic</u> and <u>Jewish</u> people who were entering the USA.

The WASPs had great influence in <u>Congress</u> (the American parliament).
As a consequence President Harding decided to place <u>strict limitations on immigration</u>, especially from <u>Eastern</u> and <u>Southern Europe</u>.
In <u>1924</u>, Congress passed an act which introduced a <u>quota system</u>.
Annual immigration was reduced from over one million to about 150 000 in 1929.

Isolationism — it's tariffic...

After the First World War, Europe had lots of <u>problems</u>, while America had <u>relatively few</u>.
By <u>limiting imports</u> and <u>reducing immigration</u>, the US sought to secure its peace and prosperity.

Prosperity in the 1920s

The 1920s were a time of <u>huge economic growth</u> in the US.

The 1920s were a Time of Plenty

This decade was a '<u>boom time</u>' for many — incomes rose and standards of living improved.

1) There was <u>low inflation</u>, <u>low unemployment</u> and <u>low interest rates</u>.
2) Cities were rebuilt with tall <u>skyscrapers</u>, and major <u>road building</u> programmes were undertaken.
3) There was a <u>consumer boom</u>. More people could now afford items such as radios, refrigerators, washing machines, vacuum cleaners and telephones.
4) <u>Advertising</u> encouraged <u>more spending</u> and became a big business in itself, expanding into radio and film commercials.
5) <u>Hire purchase</u> (buying in instalments) was introduced to make <u>cars</u> affordable to average earners who could only buy them on credit. It encouraged more spending on <u>luxury goods</u>.
6) Republican government policy contributed to prosperity. The <u>reduction</u> of <u>income tax</u> left people with more money to spend. The government also promoted <u>cheap credit</u> through the <u>Federal Reserve Board</u> (central banking system). They encouraged banks to <u>lend money</u> on easier terms, which (in the short term) contributed to the boom.

Electric Power

These major industries led the boom

Chemicals Industry

Motor Cars

The Stock Market boomed

1.5 million Americans <u>bought shares</u> in the 1920s. Before the price of shares began to rocket unrealistically in 1928, there were <u>sensible reasons</u> for buying them — people were investing in a real boom in production and consumption. It only started to go bad when people took to buying shares <u>on credit</u> in the hope of <u>selling them</u> at a profit (see p.70).

The Motor Industry led the way

1) The jobs of 1 in 12 workers were <u>linked to motor car production</u>.
2) Car production <u>boosted other industries</u> — steel, petrol, chemicals, glass and rubber.
3) Cars became more <u>affordable</u> — the Model T Ford cost less than $300.
4) Production of cars became dominated by <u>the big three companies</u> — Ford, Chrysler and General Motors.
5) Ford's factory used an <u>assembly line</u> system. It divided manufacturing tasks among a group of workers spaced alongside a <u>moving belt</u>. It made production far more <u>efficient</u>, which allowed for a huge reduction in price. By 1929, there was <u>one car</u> for every <u>five Americans</u>.

4.5m

1.9m

1920   1929

Annual car production

Boom in the US — revise this and prosper...

This page is really important. It shows you how the American economy really <u>took off</u> in the 1920s. Make sure you learn some of these <u>statistics</u> — they'll impress the examiners.

Poverty in the 1920s

While there was a boom for many Americans, for others life remained a struggle.

There was still Poverty

Wealth wasn't distributed evenly — there was a big gap between rich and poor in the USA.

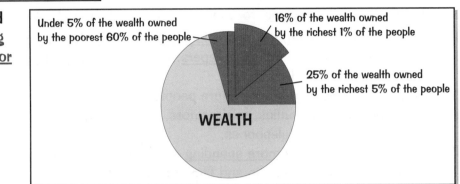

Under 5% of the wealth owned by the poorest 60% of the people

16% of the wealth owned by the richest 1% of the people

25% of the wealth owned by the richest 5% of the people

WEALTH

Some poverty was in Urban Areas

1) Monopolies (where a whole industry is owned or controlled by one company or alliance) kept prices high and wages low, by stopping competition for customers and workers.
2) Many African Americans had moved from the South to the northern states to work in war industries. They were often restricted by prejudice and poverty to living in poor districts.
3) Some urban poverty was produced by the pressure of numbers — many people moved to cities because of rural hardship.

"Old" industries Suffered

1) The coal industry did badly. Coal mining suffered from competition with oil. Cars and trucks began to take over from the railways, which were a major user of coal.
2) About 10% less coal was mined in 1929 than in 1919. More efficient mining technology also caused workers to be laid off, and those that remained saw their wages decrease. The mining towns suffered acute hardship.
3) In 1920 the wartime cotton boom collapsed. In 1921 the boll weevil — a beetle that feeds off cotton plants — destroyed 30% of the crop. In the mid 1920s the opposite problem, overproduction, caused prices to plunge.

Problems in Agriculture led to Rural Poverty

1) Farmers had prospered during the war. But during the 1920s, they grew more food than was needed. Overproduction led to falling prices and so to falling profits.
2) Taxes, mortgages and wages were rising, further reducing farmers' profits.
3) Foreign competition increased during the 1920s. European agriculture recovered from the war, while Canada, Russia, Argentina and Australia also competed on the world market.
4) The Republican government didn't believe in direct help to farmers. When Congress passed the McNary-Haugen bill, to allow the government to buy up farmers' crops, President Coolidge vetoed it twice — he thought it would encourage more overproduction.
5) For the first time ever, the American farm population began to shrink.

The Jazz Age wasn't all Bentleys and champagne...

There are always winners and losers — the 1920s were no different. It's important to remember that some people struggled through what are often thought of as the 'good times'.

Intolerance in the 1920s

Some groups in 1920s America suffered discrimination and persecution.

Prejudice against Immigrants led to the Red Scare

1) There was prejudice against newer immigrant groups and worries about communist agitators entering the country. In 1919 the authorities used a series of bombings across the country to whip up a 'Red Scare'. They deported over 4000 people, mainly Russians.

2) During the Red Scare, two Italian anarchists called Nicola Sacco and Bartolomeo Vanzetti were convicted of murder and robbery. There were protests by people who argued it was a miscarriage of justice, and that the judge was prejudiced. But they were executed in 1927.

- From 1917 immigrants had to pass a 'literacy test' to enter.
- A quota system was introduced in 1921. This was replaced in 1924 by the National Origins Act which strictly limited immigration. This act discriminated against immigrants from Southern and Eastern Europe, and Asia.

The racist Ku Klux Klan (KKK) Expanded

1) First formed in the 1860s, the Ku Klux Klan gained new popularity in the early 1920s.
2) The KKK was a white supremacist organisation based in the Southern states of the USA.
3) They opposed African Americans being given more rights. They were also prejudiced against immigrants, Jewish people and Catholics. They used intimidation and violence.
4) KKK membership had grown to around 4 million by 1925.
5) In 1925, there was a scandal involving Indiana KKK leader D.C. Stephenson (he was convicted of kidnapping and second degree murder). The organisation lost much support, and never regained such significant cultural and political power.

Some Laws were Racist

1) The 'Jim Crow Laws' was a collective name for laws that discriminated against African Americans. These were more common in the Southern states of the USA.

> **DRINKING FOUNTAIN**
> **WHITE ONLY**

2) Some laws made it difficult for African Americans to vote. For example, it was law in some states that voters had to show that their grandfathers had voted — this excluded many African Americans whose ancestors were slaves with no voting rights (slavery was only abolished in America in 1865).

3) Some laws forced white and African American people to use separate facilities, e.g. different schools, transport, parks, cafes and theatres. This was called segregation. Although the facilities were supposed to be "separate but equal", the ones provided for African Americans were usually much worse.

There was an ugly, violent side to American society...

Remember — there were many groups who were discriminated against in 1920s USA. Racist organisations grew in popularity and some new laws restricted the rights of certain people.

Prohibition and Organised Crime

In <u>January 1920</u> it became illegal to manufacture, distribute or sell alcohol. This was <u>Prohibition</u>.

In 1920 America tried to turn Teetotal

1) <u>Pressure</u> for Prohibition had built up over a <u>long time</u>. Some states were "<u>dry</u>" by 1917.
2) <u>Temperance movements</u> had been <u>campaigning</u> for Prohibition since the 19th century — they were popular in <u>rural areas</u>, and were often <u>Christian</u>. They claimed alcohol led to <u>violence</u>, <u>immoral behaviour</u>, and the <u>breakdown</u> of family life.
3) The <u>middle class</u> often blamed alcohol for <u>disorder</u> among immigrants and the working class. <u>Businessmen</u> blamed alcohol for making workers <u>unreliable</u>.
4) The First World War (which the USA joined in 1917) resulted in more support for Prohibition. Many breweries were owned by <u>German immigrants</u> — and the USA was fighting Germany.
5) <u>Opposition</u> to <u>Prohibition</u> was mainly in <u>urban</u> areas — especially cities in the northern states.

> <u>Saloons</u> were closed down. Buying alcohol illegally was <u>expensive</u>, which caused <u>consumption to decrease</u> — especially among the poor. The US authorities recruited over 1500 <u>agents</u> (later increased to 2800+) to enforce the law.

Organised Crime 'took over' the distribution of alcohol

1) <u>Millions of dollars</u> were made trading in illegal alcohol. Prohibition saw a massive rise in organised crime and gangsterism as <u>rival gangs</u> fought for control of the business.

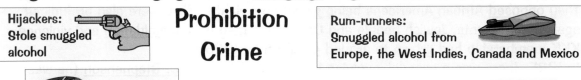

Prohibition Crime

Hijackers: Stole smuggled alcohol

Rum-runners: Smuggled alcohol from Europe, the West Indies, Canada and Mexico

Moonshiners: Made their own liquor

Speakeasies: Illegal drinking clubs sprang up with secret passwords at the door

Bootleggers: Sold on redistilled industrial alcohol

2) In Chicago 1926-29, <u>gang warfare</u> led to <u>1300 murders</u>. <u>Al Capone</u> was a gang leader:

Al Capone worked for Johnny Torrio, a leading Chicago Gangster.

Taking over from Torrio in 1925, the ruthless Capone was making $60m a year from alcohol and $45m from gambling, dance halls and race tracks.

He used a private army to intimidate voters and fight rival gangs. In 1929, 7 members of a rival gang were machine-gunned in the St Valentine's Day Massacre.

Capone was sentenced to 11 years in prison for tax evasion in 1931. In poor health, he retired to his Florida mansion and died in 1947.

Prohibition finally ended in 1933

1) Enforcing Prohibition proved impossible because there was still a <u>public demand</u> for alcohol.
2) Prohibition led to <u>corruption</u> — judges and policemen took <u>bribes</u> from gangsters. Some policemen even got involved in bootlegging themselves. In 1930, <u>George Cassiday</u>, a bootlegger, revealed that he'd sold alcohol to most of Congress (the US parliament).
3) In his 1932 presidential campaign, <u>Roosevelt</u> (see p.72) promised to <u>repeal</u> Prohibition. Congress repealed Prohibition in December <u>1933</u>.

Prohibition — a tee-total disaster...

When prohibition began, criminals quickly got involved — there was <u>big money</u> to be made.

Social Developments

American society went through lots of <u>changes</u> in the 1920s. This decade is known as the '<u>Roaring Twenties</u>' — the economy was booming and lots of people were having a good time.

Many people had More Money to spend on Leisure

Paperback books

Motor transport

Films

Radio

Jazz music clubs

New dances like the Charleston and Lindy hop

1) <u>Film</u> became the essential <u>mass entertainment</u> — and a multi-million dollar industry. Huge <u>cinemas</u> were built which could seat up to 4000 people. Films were silent until <u>1927</u>, when the first "<u>talking</u>" picture was released. <u>Hollywood</u> was the major film-making centre.

2) <u>Radio</u> also boomed. In 1921 there was just one <u>licensed station</u>. Two years later there were <u>508</u>. Millions of <u>sets</u> were sold. By 1929, $850m was spent on sets and parts every year. The <u>NBC</u> (National Broadcasting Company) was set up in 1926. By 1929 it had made $150m from <u>advertising</u>.

There were changing Manners and Morals

1) Young people enjoyed <u>smoking</u>, <u>dancing</u> and <u>cocktail parties</u>. Some women started to wear <u>lipstick</u>, <u>shorter skirts</u> and <u>high heels</u> (these women were called <u>flappers</u>).
2) Church attendance <u>fell</u> and the divorce rate <u>increased</u>.
3) But many people felt that permissiveness and <u>sexual freedom</u> had gone <u>too far</u>.

Women gained more Freedom and Independence

1) Films, popular songs and paperbacks encouraged <u>new fashions and freedom</u>.
2) Some <u>feminists</u> encouraged liberation, but had only limited success.
3) Women were encouraged to gain <u>economic independence</u> — some learned a trade or trained as typists or secretaries. New <u>office jobs</u> provided employment for many women.
4) Household <u>gadgets</u> gave some relief from <u>domestic drudgery</u>.
5) Rising high school and college attendance meant women were <u>better educated</u> than before.

But Traditional Views continued

1) Some books and magazines tried to set '<u>decent</u>' standards.
2) Women were still expected to be <u>homemakers</u>.
3) In employment there was continuing <u>discrimination against women</u>.
4) The vast majority of working class women continued in <u>low skilled, low paid jobs</u>.
5) Traditional male values continued to emphasise the <u>superiority of men</u> in the 'public sphere'.

Hollywood, short skirts — and all that jazz...

What a great couple of pages to learn here — <u>gangsters</u>, <u>flappers</u>, <u>film stars</u>, they're all here. Don't get carried away though — you still need to know all these facts in detail for the exam.

The Wall Street Crash

Wall Street is the major financial centre in New York. Stocks and shares are bought and sold there.

On Black Thursday share prices Plummeted

On Thursday 24th October 1929 around 13 million shares were sold. Confidence in the value of shares began to fall. On 28th and 29th October, a series of sharp falls began in the value of shares.

- Some major stocks lost three quarters of their value.
- Prices continued to fall for years.
- At the lowest point in 1933, 83% of the stock market's value had been lost.

Falling prices → Loss of Confidence — panic → Losses by brokers and private investors → Pressure on banks → Bankruptcy of larger corporations, closure of banks

Efforts to Shore Up prices Failed

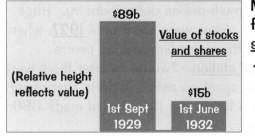

$89b — 1st Sept 1929

$15b — 1st June 1932

Value of stocks and shares

(Relative height reflects value)

Most early losers were large-scale speculators. Leading financiers met to pool $240m. They used this to buy shares in an attempt to restore confidence and stop panic.

They failed — panic selling led to further falls.
- Investment trusts were unable to meet their obligations.
- Defaulting on debts led to bankruptcy for others.
- People rushed to withdraw their savings from banks, causing many banks to go bust.

Underlying Economic Problems contributed to the Crash

Though the 1920s had been a 'boom time' for many, there were serious problems with the economy. Prosperity depended on people continuing to spend. But many people had run up large debts, or had already bought the consumer goods they needed. After 1927 there was a downturn in demand.

This situation was made even worse for a number of reasons.

1) Wealth was distributed unequally — rising profits were not passed on to workers, so most people were too poor to spend more. This meant demand did not rise as fast as production.

2) There was overproduction — industry was producing more than people wanted to buy. By 1929, unsold stock was building up and manufacturers reduced production. They started to lay off staff and unemployment increased.

3) Banks were largely unregulated. They were unstable and gambled depositors' money on the stock exchange.

4) Brokers provided expensive loans to enable investors to buy shares. When the stock market crashed, investors could not pay back their loans.

5) There were barriers to trade (such as high tariffs) between the USA and Europe — partly because of the USA's policy of isolationism (see p.64). Plus European countries had suffered economically because of the First World War. This meant Europe couldn't provide a good market for America's surplus goods.

Wall Street '29 — a crash course in things going wrong...

Speculating on the stock market means trying to make money by buying and selling shares. When it all went wrong, everybody suffered because of the awful effect on the economy...

Consequences of the Wall Street Crash

The crash <u>destroyed confidence</u>. People lost money and savings and there was no recovery in sight. A second long decline from mid-1931 to early 1933 resulted in <u>even more bankruptcies</u>.

The Depression hit all walks of life

1) Around 20 000 US <u>businesses folded</u> in 1932 alone.
2) From late 1929 to mid-1932 <u>5000 banks folded</u> — losing over $3 billion of deposits.
3) The <u>national income fell</u> from over $80b to $40b (1929-33).
4) The price of goods continued to fall. Industrial production was cut. <u>Wages fell</u> and workers were laid off. A <u>quarter of the workforce</u> (about 13 million) were <u>unemployed</u> by 1933.
5) <u>Farm product prices fell 60%</u>. It was costing farmers <u>more</u> to harvest and transport their produce than they could make by <u>selling it</u> — fruit <u>rotted</u>, sheep were <u>killed and burnt</u>, wheat was not harvested and <u>debts increased</u>. Many bankrupt farmers were <u>evicted</u> or became tenants, <u>losing their independence</u>.

The Depression caused Terrible Poverty

1) Poverty led to <u>undernourishment</u>.
2) Thousands were made <u>homeless</u>. Some of the homeless built <u>shanty towns</u> to live in. These were nicknamed <u>Hoovervilles</u> after <u>President Hoover</u>.
3) Many people <u>moved</u> to seek work. Some fathers <u>abandoned</u> their families in the search for work.
4) <u>Migrant farm workers</u> roamed the countryside looking for work. Their situation was made worse by a period of <u>drought</u> in the Midwest, partly caused by <u>overuse of the land</u>.
5) Marriages were delayed and the <u>birth rate fell</u>.

TYPICAL DIET DURING THE DEPRESSION

Breakfast
Bread and coffee

Dinner
Bread, carrots and soup

Attempts were made to Help People

The Depression was a <u>shattering</u> and <u>demoralising</u> experience. Some people fought hard for survival and to keep their <u>pride</u>. State and charitable agencies tried to help people keep going.

Private charities, religious groups → **RELIEF** → Temporary homes and shelter

State governments → **AND** → Supply of food and clothes / Bread lines and soup kitchens

Federal relief agencies → **HELP** → Offers of jobs

John Steinbeck's great novel <u>The Grapes of Wrath</u> tells the story of farmers forced to try their luck in California during the Depression. If you haven't got time to read it, try to find a copy of the film to watch — you can feel like you're revising while watching a great movie. (Don't forget to learn this stuff too though.)

From bad to worse — more than a little depressing...

The main point on this page is simply that the Depression was really bad, and made lots of people <u>destitute</u> and <u>miserable</u>. That's not enough though — you need to learn the details too.

Election of Roosevelt (FDR)

The Republican President Hoover tried to deal with the Depression — but he <u>failed</u>.

Hoover's Action on the Economy didn't go far enough

Hoover tried some measures to help the economy:
1) Some <u>reduction in taxation</u> so that people had more money to spend.
2) An expansion of '<u>public works</u>'.
3) A <u>Home Loans Act</u> to help with mortgage payments.
4) <u>Conferences</u> with <u>industrialists</u> in an effort to maintain jobs and wages.
5) A one-year <u>suspension on war debts</u> and reparations by European governments to the USA in the hope that this would enable them to buy more American goods.
6) The <u>Reconstruction Finance Corporation</u> provided some loans to help firms.

For many people this was "<u>too little, too late</u>". Hoover persisted in his belief in '<u>rugged individualism</u>' — he believed that if the right conditions could be created, people would be able to <u>work themselves out of poverty</u> without direct assistance from the government. He therefore <u>refused</u> to offer any financial <u>relief</u> to individuals. This was very <u>unpopular</u>.

Some of Hoover's policies may even have harmed the world economy and hampered US recovery. For example, <u>high tariffs on foreign goods</u> led to retaliation — other countries raised their tariffs to <u>protect</u> their <u>own industries</u>. US exports to Europe more than halved between 1929 and 1932.

FDR was Elected in 1932

1) FDR (Franklin Delano Roosevelt) had been a popular <u>governor of New York</u>. He ran a well organised and <u>energetic election campaign</u> supported by wealthy backers. Influential supporters helped him with ideas and well written speeches. So FDR looked like a winner.
2) Hoover wasn't helped by the '<u>Bonus Army</u>' protests in June 1932. 15,000 First World War army veterans gathered in Washington to demand extra bonus payments not due until 1945. Two protesters were killed by police, and many more were injured in army action to clear their encampments.
3) The <u>Democrats</u> swept to <u>power</u>, with FDR gaining 22 million votes and Hoover 15 million.

ELECTION PROMISES

Immediate action after the election

Relief and help for small banks and homeowners

A flexible approach for practical results

FDR thought that Federal Government should act and lead on the economy

Prohibition to be ended

FDR had 3 Main Aims

This was to be a '<u>New Deal</u>' for the American people.

<u>Relief</u> — to help to improve the lives of people.
<u>Recovery</u> — to begin to rebuild US industry and trade.
<u>Reform</u> — to change conditions to ensure future progress.

Happy times are here again...

The Great Depression was a terrible time. Hoover tried to help <u>big business</u> and the <u>economy as a whole</u>, but he did little to help <u>ordinary people</u>. That's why he lost to FDR in 1932.

The New Deal

Roosevelt now had to <u>deliver</u> his 'New Deal' to the American people.

Confidence had to be restored in Banking and Finance

1) There was a four-day '<u>bank holiday</u>' closure.
2) Healthy, sound banks <u>reopened</u>. <u>Weak banks</u> were reorganised under Federal supervision.
3) Laws were introduced to <u>insure deposits</u> and <u>limit speculation</u>.
4) The <u>stock market</u> was to be monitored more closely.
5) The USA was taken off the '<u>gold standard</u>'.
6) Bank failures fell — deposits rose — and <u>confidence</u> began to return.

The 'Hundred Days' Launched Many New Measures

The "<u>Hundred Days</u>" was the first period of Roosevelt's term in office, during which he introduced many new acts. Much work was carried out by special <u>Federal agencies</u> (often called '<u>alphabet agencies</u>' because they were known by their initials). The most important were:

FERA The <u>Federal Emergency Relief Administration</u> made $500m available to state and local government for emergency relief. This was used to give direct assistance to the poor, for example: for dole payments and soup kitchens.

CCC The <u>Civilian Conservation Corps</u> provided work for thousands of unemployed men in forestry, water and soil conservation projects. This was followed by the <u>Public Works Administration (PWA)</u> which provided work building roads, bridges, hospitals, schools and housing.

AAA The <u>Agricultural Adjustment Administration</u> paid farmers to limit food production. This raised prices and increased incomes. The AAA also helped farmers modernise and rebuild their businesses.

NRA The <u>National Recovery Act</u> drew up codes of fair competition, set minimum wages and a maximum eight-hour day. Trade unions were encouraged. This was a cooperative effort and relied on the voluntary agreement of business.

TVA The <u>Tennessee Valley Authority</u>. See page 74 for details.

HOLC The <u>Home Owners' Loan Corporation</u> helped people who were in danger of having their homes repossessed. It provided new long-term loans.

The Economy Strengthened a bit but Problems remained

1) Some agencies gave out money too <u>slowly</u>.
2) Stricter regulations on hours, wages and child labour <u>hurt small businesses and farmers</u>.
3) <u>Tenant farmers</u> continued to suffer — 3 million were displaced from the land (1932-5).
4) There was some <u>opposition to Federal control</u> — for example by the 'Liberty League' (1934-6). The Supreme Court raised <u>constitutional objections</u>, which delayed several of FDR's measures.
5) After an initial increase in industrial production the NRA encountered much opposition from business and was <u>unable to secure continued recovery</u>. Some argue that FDR didn't put enough money into reviving industry.
6) The <u>severe drought</u> and heat, on top of overfarming, led to the erosion of topsoil in large areas of the Midwest. Parts of Kansas and Oklahoma became '<u>dust bowls</u>'.

> But the fall in wages and prices was halted. <u>Employment</u> rose and, despite criticisms that Roosevelt was not being radical enough, the measures were very <u>popular</u>.

Learn this and you can have an ice cream — a new deal...

Roosevelt gave speeches on the radio known as '<u>fireside chats</u>'. These urged listeners to have faith in the New Deal. Overall, he gave the American public a big old charm offensive.

The TVA and the Second New Deal

There were still problems left that needed action...

The Tennessee Valley Authority (TVA)

1) The Tennessee Valley was one of the poorest regions in the country. Overcultivation had led to soil erosion and this had turned the land into a near desert.
2) Agriculture was in a dreadful condition and industry almost non-existent. Many local people were leaving the area to find work further west.

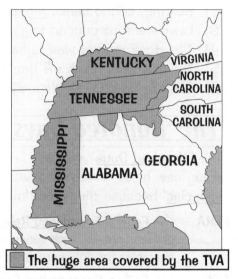

The huge area covered by the TVA

TVA brought Construction Projects

1) The TVA built a large number of dams to prevent the flooding that had been causing so much damage and to provide irrigation in times of drought.
2) Trees were planted to prevent more soil erosion.
3) The TVA constructed power stations which brought electricity to the area.

There was a huge improvement in the region's economy. The massive building projects provided thousands of jobs for local people. Agriculture began to prosper.

The Second New Deal focused on Social Welfare

The Second New Deal began in 1935 and took the new ideas about social welfare and the responsibilities of the state even further. Roosevelt introduced new measures that would benefit the elderly, the sick and the unemployed.

The Social Security Act was passed in 1935

1) This began America's state system of old age pensions. Americans over 65 received a government pension.
2) It also set up a plan for unemployment benefit. Both employers and employees paid into a fund so that the worker received a small amount of unemployment benefit if they lost their job.
3) It also set up schemes to help the sick and the disabled.

The Wagner Act, 1935

This act gave workers the right to join a trade union. Companies were now forced by law to allow their employees to become members of a trade union.

The Works Progress Administration (WPA), 1935

This was very like the Public Works Administration, but it also created jobs for actors, artists, photographers and musicians. However, the USA still lagged behind countries like Britain and Germany in social welfare provision.

A new New Deal for y'all to remember...

A big change brought about by the New Deal was the acceptance that the state had a role in relieving the hardship of individual citizens. This was what the second New Deal was all about.

Opposition to the New Deal

Although many Americans supported the New Deal, some people <u>opposed</u> Roosevelt's policies.

Some thought the New Deal had Not Gone Far Enough

1) The politician <u>Senator Huey Long</u> of Louisiana had a plan that he called '<u>Share Our Wealth</u>'.
2) Long wanted to <u>tax the rich</u> and give the money to the poor. He claimed that it would give every family an income of $5000 a year. The families would <u>spend</u> the money and this would create a bigger demand for goods and services and therefore <u>more jobs</u>.
3) Huey Long planned to stand against FDR in the 1936 <u>presidential elections</u> — but he was <u>assassinated</u> in 1935. FDR was re-elected in a <u>landslide victory</u> in the 1936 election.

1) Another of Roosevelt's critics was <u>Dr Francis Townsend</u>. Dr Townsend recommended a plan by which every American over <u>60</u> was given a <u>pension</u> of $200 per month (a huge amount in the 1930s) on condition that they spent the lot within one month.
2) Dr Townsend said that this would give a <u>big boost</u> to the economy and get <u>unemployment down</u>.

Some thought the New Deal had Gone Too Far

Some <u>businessmen</u> and the <u>Republican party</u> took the view that the New Deal had gone too far.

1) Roosevelt's critics said that the New Deal made Americans <u>too dependent on government help</u>. These people believed that it was <u>wrong</u> for the government to <u>create work</u> and give Americans pensions and sickness benefits. Individuals should provide these things for themselves through their <u>own efforts</u>.
2) Some business people were angry that the New Deal allowed <u>trade unions</u> into the <u>workplace</u>. They said this was <u>unnecessary</u> government <u>interference</u> in the way that they ran their business affairs.
3) Some people condemned the New Deal measures as '<u>socialist</u>' and therefore <u>un-American</u>.
4) It was claimed that it was <u>wrong to tax the rich</u> to pay for the New Deal. The rich had earned their wealth through their <u>own efforts</u> and <u>enterprise</u>. By taxing the rich you discouraged them from wishing to <u>create more wealth</u>. This was a strongly <u>capitalist</u> viewpoint.

There was also Opposition from the Supreme Court

1) In 1935, the Supreme Court declared that several of the New Deal measures were <u>unconstitutional</u> and therefore illegal. Most of the judges were <u>Republicans</u> and therefore opposed to Roosevelt and his policies.
2) Roosevelt asked the Congress to allow him to put six <u>Democrats</u> on the Supreme Court so that this would not happen again. However, many Americans felt that this would be a violation of the constitution and Roosevelt was <u>forced to back down</u>.
3) The Supreme Court began to take a more lenient view of the New Deal and the argument died down. However the objections did succeed in <u>delaying</u> some of FDR's policies.

Money, money, money...

America was (and to a great extent still is) attached to ideas of <u>free enterprise</u> and <u>minimal state</u> intervention in the affairs of individuals. This largely explains the opposition to FDR.

How Successful was the New Deal?

The New Deal had <u>mixed success</u> — no American president had promised anything like this before.

The New Deal really was New

1) The New Deal was a <u>new idea</u> — it was the <u>first time</u> the US government had seriously <u>intervened</u> in the US <u>economy</u> to help the poorest Americans.

2) President Hoover had favoured a more <u>traditional approach</u> — he didn't think the government should tell people how to run their businesses. He promoted the ideas of <u>self-reliance</u> and <u>cooperation</u>. He wanted people to work their <u>own way</u> out of <u>debt</u> and <u>help others</u> do the same — without relying on direct help from the government.

3) FDR was more <u>radical</u> — he thought the government should be <u>actively responsible</u> for <u>helping struggling</u> US citizens caught up in the Depression. That's why he introduced the <u>New Deal</u>.

The New Deal had considerable success in its Main Aims

Give aid to the needy

1) The <u>FERA</u> did a <u>good job</u> in providing the needy with much-needed <u>emergency aid</u>.

2) From 1935 onwards, the elements of a basic <u>welfare state</u> were established — <u>unemployment benefit</u> and <u>pensions</u> were introduced, and the government intervened to ensure better working conditions and a <u>minimum wage</u>.

Restore stability to America's banking and financial system

1) Roosevelt successfully resolved the <u>banking crisis</u> with the <u>Emergency Banking Act (EBA)</u>.

2) This <u>restored</u> people's <u>confidence</u> in the <u>banks</u> and people began to deposit their money in them once again.

Reduce unemployment and restore prosperity

1) The New Deal created <u>millions of jobs</u> through the various agencies such as the CCC and the PWA. When Roosevelt became president in 1933, unemployment stood at <u>13 million</u>. In 1940, the figure was <u>8 million</u>.

2) However, though the 1940 figure is an improvement on the one for 1933, it is important to remember that there were <u>only 1.5 million people out of work in 1929</u>. So the New Deal did not actually bring back the low unemployment levels of 1920s America.

3) In 1937, another depression hit the American economy and unemployment rose in 1938 to over 10 million. The New Deal therefore <u>failed</u> to solve America's <u>unemployment problem</u>.

World War Two solved the <u>*Unemployment Problem*</u>

It was the outbreak of the <u>Second World War</u> in Europe that brought the jobless total down.

1) From 1941 onwards the US geared production to <u>war needs</u>, eventually supplying her allies with <u>$50 billion</u> worth of food, armaments and equipment.

2) America's entry into the <u>war</u> in December 1941 <u>increased the demand</u> for military equipment. This, together with <u>recruitment</u> into the armed forces, put an end to high unemployment.

The end of the Depression — I feel better already...

Roosevelt achieved a lot, but he could only <u>relieve</u> the worst of the <u>hardship</u>. It took major changes in economic conditions, caused by the <u>Second World War</u>, to finally fix unemployment.

Revision Summary

You've read the section, now try these revision questions, just to check that you've got the whole thing stored safely in your brain. Don't forget — if you get any wrong, look back through the section, learn it properly and then try again...

1) Who became President in 1921?
2) What did the Fordney-McCumber Tariff allow the US President to do?
3) How did the Republican government's policies encourage the economic boom in the 1920s?
4) Explain how the motor industry contributed to American prosperity in the 1920s.
5) Why did agriculture not share in the boom?
6) Why were there protests about the trial of Sacco and Vanzetti?
7) What did the Ku Klux Klan believe in? Who did they persecute?
8) When was Prohibition introduced?
9) Explain the following terms: speakeasy, rum-running, moonshine.
10) What crime was Al Capone convicted of in 1931?
11) Name three forms of entertainment which first became popular in the 1920s.
12) Explain how the social position of women changed in the 1920s.
13) What year did the Wall Street Crash happen?
14) Explain four economic problems that contributed to the Wall Street Crash.
15) How many Americans were unemployed by 1933?
16) What were Hoovervilles?
17) Explain why Hoover lost the 1932 election.
18) Who won the 1932 election? What were his three main aims?
19) Name three 'alphabet agencies' and explain how they helped America through the Depression.
20) What does TVA stand for?
21) Name two acts passed in 1935 as part of the 'Second New Deal'.
22) Why did Huey Long oppose the New Deal?
23) Explain why some businessmen and members of the Republican party opposed the New Deal.
24) How successful was the New Deal in achieving its three main aims?
25) What finally solved America's unemployment problem?

The Great Powers in Europe 1900

To really get to grips with <u>why the war started</u>, you'll need to know about the background to it.

There were Five main Rival Nations in Europe

1) **BRITAIN** ruled an empire of over <u>one quarter</u> of the world's people, and owned <u>rich industries</u>. Britain was an island, so it had a <u>strong navy</u> to protect itself and its colonies from invasion. During the 19th century, Britain had followed a policy of <u>'splendid isolation'</u> — it didn't get involved in European politics.

2) **FRANCE** also had an <u>overseas</u> empire. The French were <u>bitter</u> about losing Alsace and Lorraine to Germany in the Franco-Prussian War in 1871.

3) **RUSSIA** was poor, but the <u>biggest country</u> in Europe. It was ruled by Tsar Nicholas II. It had <u>no lands</u> overseas, but wanted land in Europe and Asia with <u>access</u> to the <u>sea</u>.

4) **AUSTRIA-HUNGARY** was a central European empire, made up of 10 different nationalities — many of whom wanted <u>independence</u>. It was ruled by the Emperor Franz Joseph I.

5) **GERMANY** had a <u>small empire</u> ruled by Kaiser Wilhelm II. The Kaiser was <u>jealous</u> of Britain's superior <u>sea power</u> and rich colonies. He wanted to increase German influence and wealth abroad. The Kaiser described Germany's small empire as its <u>'place in the sun'</u>, and was keen to expand it.

BRITAIN	185 warships
	700 000 men
FRANCE	62 warships
	1 000 000 men
RUSSIA	30 warships
	1 200 000 men
AUSTRIA-HUNGARY	28 warships
	800 000 men
GERMANY	100 warships
	2 000 000 men

Approx. sizes of European Armies and Navies in 1914

Alliances were formed for Security

Countries often made agreements to help each other out.

1) 1879: <u>Dual Alliance</u> between Germany and Austria-Hungary.

2) 1882: <u>Triple Alliance</u> when Italy joined the Dual Alliance.

These alliances created a large group of allies in <u>Central Europe</u> — making both <u>France</u> and <u>Russia</u> nervous.

3) 1892: <u>Franco-Russian Alliance</u> against the Triple Alliance.

4) 1904: <u>Entente Cordiale</u> between Britain and France.

5) 1907: The <u>Anglo-Russian Entente</u> completes the <u>Triple Entente</u> between Russia, Britain and France.

These ententes were <u>not military agreements</u> — but they ended up involving the military because of the tensions between the Triple Alliance and the Triple Entente.

These alliances and ententes created <u>more tension</u> between the major powers. Germany, Austria-Hungary and Italy felt <u>threatened</u> and <u>surrounded</u> by the Triple Entente. <u>Russia</u> was worried about <u>Austria's intentions</u> towards the Balkans. Meanwhile, <u>Britain</u> and <u>Germany</u> competed to build the <u>best navy</u> in the world...

Kaiser Wilhelm II

International politics — a sneaky business...

Countries make <u>alliances</u> with nations who share their ideas. It's also a way of <u>ganging up</u> on enemies. <u>Scribble</u> a list of the <u>main strengths</u> of these countries and the <u>alliances</u> they formed.

Tension Builds — 1900-1914

Europe was drifting towards a <u>major war</u> — and Germany and Britain played a big part.

Germany and Britain began an Arms Race

1) The Kaiser wanted Germany to be a <u>major world power</u>, but he needed a <u>bigger navy</u>. Germany began to follow a policy known as '<u>Weltpolitik</u>' — a more <u>aggressive</u> foreign policy aimed at increasing <u>military strength</u> and expanding <u>Germany's empire</u>.

2) Between 1900 and 1914 Germany attempted to <u>double the size</u> of its Navy.

3) Britain had a policy called the <u>Two Power Standard</u> — the Royal Navy always had to be as big as the <u>next two</u> strongest navies in Europe <u>put together</u>. It meant Britain would <u>never</u> be outnumbered at sea.

4) Britain <u>responded</u> to Germany's improvements in 1906 by building the first <u>Dreadnought</u> — a new and superior kind of battleship.

5) Germany built its <u>own version</u> in 1907-8 — but, by 1912, Britain had a new, <u>bigger kind</u>.

6) By 1914 Britain had <u>29</u> Dreadnoughts and Germany had <u>17</u>.

The Major Powers made Plans for War

1) Faced with enemies on both its eastern and western borders, Germany came up with the <u>Schlieffen Plan</u> in 1905. The plan was that in a war, Germany could <u>defeat France</u> before Russia mobilised, and then <u>fight Russia</u> afterwards.

2) France prepared <u>Plan 17</u> to recapture Alsace and Lorraine from Germany.

3) Britain created the <u>British Expeditionary Force</u> (<u>BEF</u>) of 150,000 men, ready to travel immediately to Europe in case of war. The <u>Territorial Army</u> was also set up.

4) Russia started to <u>build up</u> its army in 1909 in case of war.

There were Two Crises over Morocco

The Moroccan Crisis 1905-6

1) Morocco was an <u>uncolonised</u> African country, but France wanted to <u>add</u> it to its empire.

2) Germany <u>objected</u> — and demanded an <u>international conference</u> on Morocco's future.

3) At the <u>Algeciras Conference</u> in 1906, Germany was forced to <u>back down</u> by British, Italian, Russian and Spanish <u>support</u> for France taking control of Morocco's police and banks.

The Agadir Crisis 1911

1) The French <u>sent troops</u> to Fez to fight Moroccan rebels.

2) Germany <u>accused</u> France of trying to take complete control over Morocco.

3) Germany <u>sent a warship</u> called the <u>Panther</u> to Agadir, hoping to <u>force France</u> to give them the French Congo.

4) Britain was worried that Germany might build a <u>naval base</u> at Agadir, which would <u>threaten</u> key British sea routes — so Britain <u>also sent</u> warships.

5) Germany <u>backed down</u> and recognised French influence in Morocco. The Germans felt increasingly <u>anti-British</u>.

Countdown to conflict — only a matter of time...

There you go then, three major factors in the start of the First World War. As soon as the <u>arms race</u> began, it was clear a war was possible — Germany was trying to overtake British power.

Section 7 — Causes and Events of the First World War

Trouble in the Balkans

The Balkans were known as 'the powder keg of Europe' — a spark of trouble could mean chaos.

The Balkans were Controlled by the Turkish Empire

1) The Balkans were a very poor area of south-eastern Europe.
2) The Turkish Empire (also known as the Ottoman Empire) was very weak. It suffered from increasing corruption and the rise of nationalism among many of the countries it controlled. People called it 'the Sick Man of Europe'.

The Balkans 1912 (before the First Balkan War)

Other powers wanted Influence

1) GERMANY wanted to build a railway to the East through the Balkans.
2) AUSTRIA-HUNGARY wanted to stop Serbia from stirring up the Slavic people inside its own lands. The Slavs wanted independence and hoped Serbia (a Slavic country) would help them.
3) RUSSIA is also a Slavic country. It wanted sea access from the Black Sea to the Mediterranean, through straits controlled by the Turkish Empire.
4) ITALY wanted to control the other side of the Adriatic Sea.

In 1908 Austria-Hungary annexed Bosnia & Herzegovina

1) Austria-Hungary had been given control of Bosnia by an 1878 treaty. They wanted to make it an official part of their empire. They cut a deal with Russia — who would support this 'annexation' if Austria-Hungary backed Russian hopes of getting access for its warships through the Turkish Straits.
2) Russia didn't get what it wanted, as other powers stood against it — but Austria-Hungary went ahead with the annexation. Russia protested, but Germany, Austria-Hungary's ally, backed them. Russia wasn't strong enough to intervene against them both. This left Russia feeling angry and humiliated.

Two Wars created more tensions

The First Balkan War

Greece, Bulgaria, Serbia and Montenegro formed the Balkan League and attacked the Turkish Empire in 1912. The Turks were beaten easily and were driven out of the Balkan area and forced to give up their lands.

The Second Balkan War

In 1913 the Balkan League quarrelled — Bulgaria went to war with Greece and Serbia. Turkey and Romania joined the Greek and Serbian side, and Bulgaria was soon defeated — losing land to the four victors.

The Balkans after the Second Balkan War (note increased size of Serbia)

In both of these wars, the British tried to keep the peace, instead of supporting Russia, who were on Serbia's side. Germany saw this as a sign that the Triple Entente was weak.

There'll be more trouble in the Balkans...

Tension in the Balkans was a main cause of World War One. The Slav question is key here — Serbia wanted to unite the Slavs in the region and was angry about the annexation of Bosnia.

The Outbreak of War

Tension suddenly exploded into the First World War — and it began in the Balkans.

The Black Hand was a Serbian Nationalist Group

1) The Black Hand was started in Serbia with the aim of uniting all the Serbian peoples.
2) Austria-Hungary had many Serbian citizens and feared a rebellion in its lands, especially in Bosnia.

Franz Ferdinand's Assassination spelled trouble

Archduke Franz Ferdinand was the heir to the Austro-Hungarian throne. He went to Bosnia to try to strengthen the loyalty of the Bosnian people to Austria-Hungary.

Princip - The Serbian student who shot the heir to the Austro-Hungarian throne

Dimitrijevic - Leader of the Black Hand

The Archduke was killed by a Serb student called Princip in Sarajevo in June 1914.
Princip was a Black Hand member — Austria was furious.

Events Moved Quickly towards War

The sequence of events is important. Also remember the Triple Alliance and the Triple Entente (see p.78) because they determined how the two sides shaped up for World War I.

23 JULY	Austria-Hungary blames the Serbian government for the assassination, demanding compensation and the right to send troops into Serbia.
28 JULY	Serbia refuses to let these troops in.
	Austria-Hungary declares war on Serbia and shells Belgrade.
29 JULY	Russia begins mobilising troops ready to help Serbia.
30 JULY	Germany demands that Russia stop mobilising.
1 AUGUST	Russia refuses. Germany declares war on Russia.
2 AUGUST	France begins mobilising to help Russia.
3 AUGUST	Germany declares war on France.
4 AUGUST	Germany sends troops through Belgium to attack France, following the Schlieffen Plan. Belgium is neutral, and Britain has agreed to protect Belgium. Britain orders Germany to withdraw. Germany refuses. Britain declares war on Germany.
6 AUGUST	Austria-Hungary declares war on Russia.

Now count the number of days in which all this happened — not much time for sensible thinking.

The First World War — everybody got sucked in...

I know, it's all a bit complicated. Make sure you know the sequence of events and how the alliance system meant Russia helped Serbia, so Germany helped Austria-Hungary, etc., etc...

The Schlieffen Plan

Germany faced war on both its <u>eastern</u> and <u>western</u> borders. It had a plan to quickly beat <u>France</u> by going through Belgium, before facing <u>Russia</u>. But things didn't go quite to plan.

The Germans had to Fight France and Russia

1) <u>France</u> had been defeated by Germany in 1870-71 and wanted revenge. The French had a secret plan — <u>Plan 17</u> — to take back lands they had lost in 1871 — Alsace and Lorraine.

2) France had made a <u>treaty with Russia</u>, so <u>Germany</u> expected a Russian attack from the East to help France.

3) Germany would therefore have to fight on <u>two fronts at once</u>. The answer was the <u>Schlieffen Plan</u>, thought up in 1905.

> The <u>SCHLIEFFEN PLAN</u> aimed to attack and <u>defeat France</u> through Belgium before the Russians were ready, then <u>turn back</u> to fight the <u>Russian Army</u>.

The Schlieffen Plan 1905 — what the Germans wanted...

... and what they actually got

The Schlieffen Plan Didn't Work...

1) <u>Belgium refused</u> to let the German army through to attack France. So Germany had to use <u>force</u>, which delayed their advance.

2) <u>Britain</u> had signed a treaty with Belgium in 1839 to <u>protect</u> it as a <u>neutral country</u>. When Germany <u>refused</u> to withdraw from Belgium, Britain declared war.

3) <u>Russia</u> was ready for war <u>quicker</u> than the Germans had expected. Many valuable German troops had to march East to face them <u>instead</u> of pushing on into France.

A short period of Open Warfare followed

The early <u>battles</u> of the war in the West saw the two sides struggle for an advantage:

MONS — August 1914 — the <u>British Expeditionary Force</u> (BEF) — the first troops sent over from Britain — managed to slow down the German advance, but they didn't stop it. The German Kaiser is said to have called them a '<u>contemptible little army</u>'.

MARNE — the Allied troops managed to <u>save Paris</u>, and forced the Germans to pull back to the river Aisne. The battle lasted five days.

YPRES — where both sides '<u>dashed to the sea</u>' to stop the other side controlling the coastline. The Allied troops managed it, but with a terrible <u>loss of life</u>.

> Neither side could push the other back, so they dug <u>trenches</u> to stop the enemy advancing further. By the end of 1914, the trench lines stretched all the way from the Belgian coast down to Switzerland and the two armies had reached a <u>stalemate</u>.

Get all these facts en-trenched in your brain...

Once the armies were stuck in the trenches, there was no hope of it being <u>over by Christmas</u>.

Stalemate in the West

The First World War began a <u>new type of warfare</u> — and it was shockingly horrible.

Changes in Warfare meant Stalemate in the Trenches

1) <u>Nobody</u> was used to <u>trench warfare</u>. It took a long time to work out how to <u>break</u> the stalemate.

2) No-one had commanded such <u>huge armies</u> before. They had to learn how.

3) It took <u>time</u> to train all the new soldiers. This was especially hard for the <u>British</u> who had had a small army before the war.

4) <u>New weapons</u> the armies had were better for <u>defence</u> than attack (see diagram).

5) Advancing troops <u>couldn't</u> hold on to the ground they won, and were pushed back.

Aircraft Developed

Grenades and Mines

More powerful artillery

The Machine Gun

Gas warfare (from 1915)

The end of the Cavalry Charge

The Tank (from 1916)

6) Both sides were <u>well supplied</u>, and could always call up more arms and men.

7) <u>Conditions</u> were often appalling — <u>muddy</u> and <u>wet</u> — not suited for quick attacks.

8) <u>Artillery bombardments</u> were supposed to weaken enemy lines — but they just <u>warned</u> the enemy an attack was coming.

The Generals Kept Sending Troops 'Over the Top'

<u>Both sides</u> often tried to break the deadlock by sending thousands of men across <u>No Man's Land</u>. The result was <u>huge slaughter</u> of infantry. But some battles did affect the whole war:

1) At the 2nd battle of <u>Ypres</u> in 1915, the Germans first used poison gas against the Allied troops.

2) At <u>Verdun</u> in 1916, the French, under General Petain, held the Germans back from the city.

3) This victory for France <u>boosted</u> French morale — Verdun became a symbol of French freedom and <u>demoralised</u> the Germans, who were sure it would fall.

4) In order to relieve the pressure on Verdun, the British began a <u>major attack</u> at the <u>Somme</u> (July-November 1916). At this battle the British army used a new invention — the <u>tank</u>.

The Somme was a Major Battle and a Major Disaster

<u>The Somme</u> was one of the <u>key</u> battles of the war. The British commander was <u>Sir Douglas Haig</u>. After a massive artillery bombardment, the British soldiers were sent 'over the top' to charge the German trenches. They were under orders to advance slowly, not run. This gave the Germans time to get ready for the attack. The slow-moving British soldiers were an easy target. 57 000 Britons were <u>killed</u> or <u>wounded</u> on the first day alone. Later attacks were more successful, but the battle dragged on till November. Only about 12 km of land was gained in some places.

Trench Warfare — All quiet on the Western Front...

Phew, there's a lot for you to learn here. Have a go at covering the page and scribbling down everything you can remember about it. Then check what you missed, and <u>do it again</u>.

Life in the Trenches

The Somme made it clear that <u>neither side</u> would win a breakthrough in this new kind of war.

The Results of the Battle of the Somme

1) The <u>Germans</u> had found out about the offensive on the Somme <u>before</u> it happened, which meant that there was a <u>big</u> problem with keeping military secrets.
2) The <u>British artillery</u> had <u>failed</u> to break the enemy lines. It didn't even destroy their barbed wire, despite bombarding for several days.
3) The battle was <u>filmed</u> and shown back home. It gave people some idea of what the trenches were <u>really like</u> — but some footage was <u>faked</u> because the real battle was too horrific.
4) People at home started to openly <u>criticise</u> the generals and their tactics.

Life in the Trenches was Hard and Dangerous

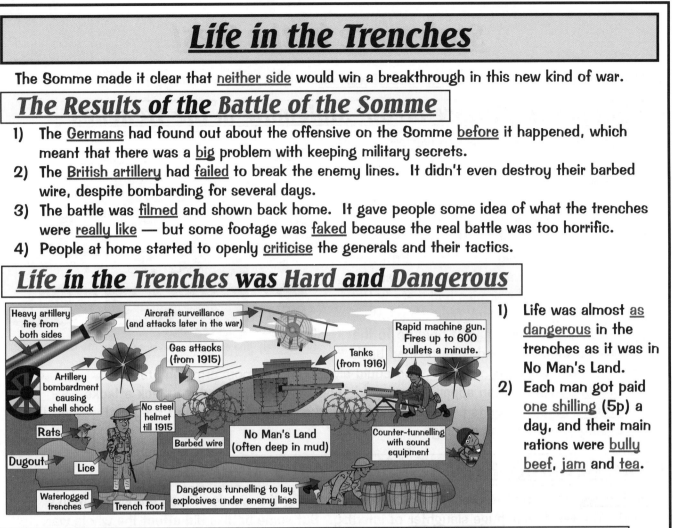

1) Life was almost <u>as dangerous</u> in the trenches as it was in No Man's Land.
2) Each man got paid <u>one shilling</u> (5p) a day, and their main rations were <u>bully beef</u>, <u>jam</u> and <u>tea</u>.

People Still Can't Agree whether the Tactics were Right

Many people <u>nowadays</u> still feel that the tactics used at the Somme and in other battles were <u>wrong</u>. Their picture of the First World War comes from <u>TV, books and films</u> — which often lay a lot of blame on Sir Douglas Haig, the "Butcher of the Somme". But in fact, it's much <u>more complicated</u> than that. Here are some of the <u>main opinions</u> on both sides.

Arguments <u>supporting</u> Haig's tactics

- Haig's main <u>aim</u> was to <u>win</u> the war, <u>whatever the cost</u> — not to save lives.
- If the <u>British government</u> at the time had thought there was a better strategy, they could have replaced Haig — but they didn't.
- Some of <u>Germany's best troops</u> were <u>killed</u> at the Somme — and couldn't be replaced.
- Haig couldn't wait for more tanks before the Somme — he had to <u>relieve the pressure</u> on <u>Verdun</u>, or the whole war might be lost.
- By 1918, Haig had learnt to <u>adapt</u> these attacking tactics so that they became more <u>successful</u>. In 1918 the British pushed the Germans back at the Battle of Amiens.

Arguments <u>against</u> Haig's tactics

- <u>Hundreds of thousands</u> of men were <u>killed</u> under Haig's command. He is quoted as saying, "The attacks are to be pressed, regardless of loss."
- Haig could have <u>waited</u> for <u>more tanks</u> at the Somme, which might have saved many lives.
- Once he saw the first day's slaughter at the Somme, he could have <u>changed tactics</u>.
- Haig could have learnt from his mistakes sooner. Instead he stuck to <u>old-fashioned ideas</u> about war that had already been shown to be disastrous — costing many lives.
- Some junior officers claimed that Haig didn't take account of <u>bad weather conditions</u>.

Trying to win the war — at a huge cost...

Opinions on the <u>British tactics</u> are a tricky business. You've really got to watch out for people just repeating <u>modern ideas</u> about Haig. Make sure you learn the main opinions on <u>both sides</u>.

New Weapons

New weapons were used in the First World War. Not surprisingly they made a <u>massive difference</u> to the way wars were fought. That's what you've got to learn about.

Aircraft were Developed throughout the war

1) On the Western Front <u>both sides</u> used <u>planes and balloons</u> to find <u>enemy weak points</u> to attack.
2) <u>The Germans</u> used airships called <u>Zeppelins</u> to carry out bombing raids like the <u>May 1915</u> one on London.
3) In <u>1915</u> new planes carried <u>synchronised</u> machine guns which <u>wouldn't</u> shoot the propeller. <u>One man</u> could fly <u>and</u> handle the gun — where before they'd needed <u>two people</u>. Fighter planes <u>escorted bombers</u> on raids, <u>attacked</u> enemy bombers, and <u>fought each other</u>, especially on the Western Front.
4) Both sides developed <u>planes</u> for <u>long-distance</u> bombing raids. The first serious raid on Britain was in <u>May 1917</u> — 71 people were killed at <u>Folkestone</u>. Britain sent bombers into <u>Germany</u> too.

Tanks made it easier to attack on the Ground

The <u>tracks</u> on tanks meant they could go over very <u>rough ground</u>, and plough through <u>barbed wire</u> without problems. The <u>heavily armoured</u> body of the tanks meant ordinary gunfire couldn't stop them. Tanks <u>should</u> have allowed the British army to break the deadlock on the trenches, but it took a while to develop effective tactics, and the early tanks often broke down.

1) The first time tanks were used was at the <u>Battle of the Somme</u> in <u>July 1916</u>. Sir Douglas Haig sent in <u>49 tanks</u>. He could have waited for more, but he decided it was more important to <u>surprise</u> the Germans, and went ahead anyway. The tank division captured <u>2 km</u> of German-held territory but <u>couldn't</u> hold on to it.
2) At <u>Cambrai</u> on the Western Front in <u>November 1917</u>, tanks were used more successfully. Nearly <u>500</u> tanks advanced about <u>6 km</u> into German territory, but <u>again</u> couldn't hold on to their gains.

Poison Gas was a deadly weapon

1) The Germans were the first to use <u>chlorine</u> gas — in the <u>Second Battle of Ypres</u>, <u>April-May 1915</u>. It caused <u>terror</u>, and killed many. The British tried it at the <u>Battle of Loos</u> (<u>September 1915</u>) but the wind blew some of it back on them. Chlorine has the military disadvantage of being <u>highly visible</u>.
2) In <u>December 1915</u> the Germans tried <u>phosgene</u>, which is <u>invisible</u> and <u>deadly</u> but <u>slow-acting</u>. At the battle of Riga, in <u>September 1917</u>, they introduced <u>mustard gas</u>, which causes horrible <u>blisters</u> and <u>internal bleeding</u>.
3) Gas became a standard weapon used by both sides, not a <u>war-winning weapon</u>. Countermeasures like <u>masks</u>, <u>pads</u> and <u>gas helmets</u> meant few British battle losses were due to gas.

New technology — it changed warfare for ever...

The development of <u>aeroplanes</u> and <u>tanks</u> as <u>weapons</u> is one of the most important <u>long-term effects</u> of the First World War. Draw a <u>timeline</u> for each weapon, giving <u>dates</u> for the main events.

Section 7 — Causes and Events of the First World War

The Eastern Front

There wasn't just a Western Front... This was a <u>world war</u>, and you've got to know about the <u>Eastern Front</u> as well.

The Russian Army was Supposed to be a Steamroller

1) The <u>Allied plan</u> was for Britain and France to hold the German army up in the West, while the Russian army advanced from the East. This would <u>trap</u> the Germans between their enemies.

2) At the start of the war, British newspapers talked confidently about the <u>Russian steamroller</u> crushing opposition as it advanced into Germany. It <u>didn't</u> happen.

3) On the other hand, the Russians <u>did</u> catch the Germans out — they were ready in just <u>10 days</u> with <u>6 million men</u>. The Germans had to <u>send troops</u> East <u>before</u> they'd defeated France — so the Schlieffen Plan had <u>failed</u>.

But the Russian Advance was a Failure

1) The Russian army <u>advanced</u> into Germany, but they <u>didn't</u> have enough <u>weapons</u>. Many soldiers had to wait for someone to be killed so that they could get hold of a rifle.

2) The Russian plans were <u>rushed</u> because of the need to advance quickly. They <u>weren't prepared</u> for a long campaign.

3) The army was <u>poorly organised</u>. Many officers were inexperienced and discipline was poor.

4) 150 000 Russians were <u>slaughtered</u> in 1914 at the battles of <u>Tannenberg</u> and the <u>Masurian Lakes</u> by German troops under von Hindenburg and Ludendorff.

5) After this the Russians were <u>driven back</u>, and the Germans and Austro-Hungarians advanced.

6) A <u>stalemate</u> soon developed on the Eastern Front. The war was now like a chess match. The war effort put a <u>great strain</u> on Russia, as civilians went hungry so the troops could be supplied.

German advance

Russian advance

The Russian steamroller — it soon ran out of steam...

There you are then, just two key facts to learn here — what the Russians were <u>supposed</u> to do and what <u>really happened</u>. Remember — because the Russians were <u>ready</u> for war quickly the Schlieffen Plan <u>failed</u>. Scribble a list of reasons why the Russian advance was such a <u>disaster</u>.

The Gallipoli Campaign

The Ottoman Empire — which was centred on Turkey — was another enemy of the Allies.

The British Planned to Weaken Germany by Attacking Turkey

1) The Ottoman Empire had joined the war on the German side in November 1914. It attacked Russia in the hope of regaining a hold in the Balkans (see p.80).
2) Some leaders in Britain like Winston Churchill, the First Lord of the Admiralty, thought that Germany and Austria-Hungary could be weakened by attacking Turkey in the East.

The Plan was to Gain Control of the Dardanelles

1) Turkey controlled the Dardanelles — the narrow entrance to the Black Sea — and this was stopping Britain getting supplies through to Russia.
2) If Britain could land troops on the Gallipoli Peninsula they could take the Dardanelles, and then go on to take Constantinople, the capital of the Turkish empire.
3) Then other nearby countries like Greece and Romania might join in on Britain's side, and help the Allies to win the war, by attacking Germany from the East.

Slaughter on the Beaches — Gallipoli 1915

1) In February, the Navy tried to advance up the Dardanelles but failed to get past the Turkish forts and mines.
2) The Navy pulled out and the Army was sent in. The force was made up of one British division and ANZAC (Australian and New Zealand Army Corps) and French troops.
3) The idea was to cross the Gallipoli peninsula and capture the Turkish capital Constantinople. The land assault began in April.
4) The Turks were ready. By firing down from hills above the beaches the Turks stopped the Allies from advancing at all.
5) The Allied side were forced to dig trenches.
6) They spent the summer and autumn under fire, suffering from heat and disease, with poor supplies of food and ammunition. There were 40 000 casualties by August.
7) It wasn't till December that the evacuation began. 105 000 soldiers were withdrawn.
8) The Turks lost even more men than the Allies: 65 000 died. This seriously weakened their army, but it wasn't obvious at the time. In December 1915 it just looked like a complete mess.

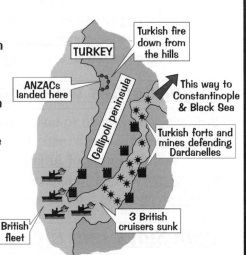

The Disaster was partly caused by Bad Planning

1) The Allied commanders didn't know the area, and didn't have proper maps.
2) They hadn't realised how strong and well-positioned the Turkish forces would be.
3) The chosen landing place was in difficult terrain — a narrow beach backed by steep hills.

Over a third of the ANZACs sent to Gallipoli died. Churchill was removed from his post as First Lord of the Admiralty, and the Dardanelles remained under Turkish control.

It wasn't just the Western Front that had trench warfare...

Complicated stuff here and there's no way round it — you've got to learn what the Gallipoli campaign tried to achieve and why it went so horribly wrong.

The War at Sea

Blockades were more important than sea battles — stopping supplies getting to Germany.

The British Navy had Four Important Jobs

1) To protect trade ships so that the Allies could remain supplied.
2) To blockade ports, preventing the enemy being supplied.
3) To carry troops to wherever they were needed.
4) To protect British colonies overseas.

The U-Boat Changed the War at Sea

1) The U-Boat was a type of German submarine. It could attack ships without being detected.
2) From 1915, thousands of tons of merchant shipping was attacked and sunk, even though Germany only had around 20 U-Boats.

Sinking of passenger ship Lusitania in 1915 — 1198 people killed, including many Americans. America outraged.

Q-ships — British warships disguised as merchant ships to attack submarines

Convoy system introduced by Lloyd George. Merchants sailed in large numbers, guarded by warships

Huge minefields laid in the English Channel

Millions of tons of shipping lost

Depth charges developed

Britain had 6 weeks' supply of wheat left in 1917

USA joined the war in 1917

Effects of the U-Boat Campaign

3) At first the Germans were careful not to attack ships from neutral countries or passenger liners. But the British realised this and began sending supplies on passenger liners too.
4) U-Boats started to attack non-military ships too — e.g. sinking the liner Lusitania in 1915.

Major Battles were Too Risky

Both sides had raced to build Dreadnoughts — (see p.79). But neither side wanted to risk these expensive ships in too many big battles. The only large-scale battle between the Dreadnought fleets was the Battle of Jutland in May 1916. Around 250 ships clashed. The German Admiral von Scheer wanted to lure part of the British fleet out of their base to attack them. But more British ships came than he expected...

Both Sides said they won at the Battle of Jutland...

1) The British lost 14 ships, and the Germans 11.
2) They fought in the evening, when it was misty, so neither side could fire accurately.
3) The British ships generally suffered more damage than the Germans.
4) The German ships and firepower seemed stronger.
5) But the German fleet left the battle first, and never put to sea in any strength after that.

Meanwhile the U-Boat Seemed to be an Unstoppable Force

1) Over 0.5 million tons of shipping was sunk in April 1917 alone.
2) The U-Boat campaign was trying to starve Britain into submission.
3) To tackle this problem, Lloyd George introduced the Convoy System — where merchant ships travelled together in groups protected by warships — to keep Britain's supplies coming in.

The war at sea — sailing to victory...

Loads of facts here — but don't let that put you off. Just make sure you learn the four jobs of the Navy, the reasons for avoiding major battles, and the effects of the U-Boat threat.

The End of the Fighting

The Russians withdrew from the fighting — but the USA joined.

Russia Pulled Out of the War in 1917

1) Tsar Nicholas II of Russia was a poor military commander.
2) To the south, the Brusilov Offensive advanced successfully into Austria-Hungary in June 1916, but was soon pushed back.
3) There was widespread starvation in the winter of 1916. Nicholas II was forced out of power in 1917 and the new Provisional Government continued the war, but was no more successful.
4) The Bolshevik Revolution in 1917 brought new leaders to power who decided to end the fighting. Russia signed the Treaty of Brest-Litovsk with Germany in 1918, giving Germany control of a large amount of Eastern territory in return for peace.
5) Two important results of Russia leaving the war were:
   i) The Allies were left to fight on without Russian help on an Eastern Front.
   ii) Germany was now able to pull back 1 million men to the Western Front.

In April 1917 the USA joined the Allies

1) In April 1917 the USA joined the war for two main reasons — the effects of the U-Boat campaign (100 American citizens were killed when the Lusitania was sunk in 1915), and a German attempt to encourage Mexico to attack the USA. This was a direct threat.
2) By now the fighting in Europe had become even fiercer. The French under General Nivelle had failed to push the Germans back.
3) The Allies fought the battles of Passchendaele and Cambrai in 1917. (The Battle of Passchendaele was also known as the Third Battle of Ypres — over 300 000 Allied troops were killed or wounded to win a few hundred metres of mud.)

Germany had to Attack Before all the Americans Arrived

Germans advancing too fast for their supplies

Trench lines

Allies able to attack at the sides

Paris

→ German attack March 1918

→ Allied forces July 1918

The River Marne

1) The USA wasn't ready to send all its troops, so Germany made a last effort to break through.
2) The Ludendorff Offensive tried to capture Paris in March 1918. It looked like it would work at first — but the Germans advanced too far too fast, and their supplies had not kept up with them.
3) They were beyond their lines in a kind of bulge, so the Allies attacked them from the flanks (sides).
4) Thousands of American troops were soon joining the Allies, and the Germans were pushed back.
5) Conditions for civilians in Germany were harsh with severe food shortages.
6) Kaiser Wilhelm II abdicated and the new government agreed a ceasefire or armistice on November 11th 1918.

US and them — America made all the difference...

Here you go, three key events in the last two years of the war — Russia's withdrawal, the USA joining the struggle and Germany trying a final big offensive. It's important to learn them NOW.

Revision Summary

Time for the best part of every section — the page with those fab revision questions to see how much you remember. I know it's a bit boring, but it's something you've got to do. It'll help you learn everything in the section — which you'll be really grateful for when you're sat in the exam. When you've finished the questions, check the answers you weren't sure about. Then have another go...

1) Which of the Great Powers had the biggest empire in the world in 1900?

2) Which two bits of land had France lost to Germany in 1871?

3) Who ruled over Germany in the run-up to World War I?

4) Which of the major powers had (1) the largest navy? (2) the largest army?

5) List the key alliances between 1882 and 1907 which split the major powers into two opposing camps.

6) Name the type of battleship which figured strongly in the naval arms race.

7) What dispute was settled by the Algeciras Conference in 1906?

8) Write a paragraph on the Agadir Crisis of 1911.

9) What was the nickname given to the Turkish Empire to show its weakness?

10) Give the reasons why Germany, Austria-Hungary, Russia and Italy all wanted influence in the Balkans at this time.

11) What did Austria-Hungary do in the Balkans in 1908? Why was it potentially so serious?

12) What was the First Balkan War about? When did it happen?

13) What happened in the Second Balkan War? How did this leave Serbia?

14) Who were the Black Hand? What did they want to achieve?

15) Who was the heir to the Austro-Hungarian throne at the time? Where was he visiting in June 1914? What happened to him there?

16) What did Austria demand from Serbia after the assassination?

17) How did Russia help Serbia after the assassination?

18) What was Germany's reaction to Russia's action?

19) What did France do after Germany's declaration of war on Russia?

20) Why did Britain decide to declare war on Germany?

21) How many days passed between Austria-Hungary's demand to Serbia and Britain's declaration of war on Germany?

22) What was the Schlieffen Plan? How was it supposed to work?

23) What was the reason for the British attack on the Somme?

24) Give two reasons why some people say Haig's tactics at the Somme were wrong.

25) Give two reasons why some people say Haig's tactics at the Somme were right.

26) Describe two ways aircraft were used during the war.

27) Give three reasons why the Russian advance on the Eastern Front was a failure.

28) Why did the Gallipoli campaign fail?

29) Give two reasons why the U-Boats caused Britain so many problems.

30) Give two reasons why the USA joined the war in 1917.

The Impact of the Cold War

The Cold War was a long period of hostility between the USA and USSR after 1945. No direct fighting took place between the two sides — but the situation was very tense.

The USA and USSR became Rivals after World War 2

1) The USA and USSR were allies during the Second World War. After the war, they were the two biggest powers in the world — often called superpowers. They soon became rivals.
2) Ideologically, they were very different. The USA was capitalist. The USSR was communist.

Early events in the Cold War

1) In the aftermath of the war, the USSR developed a sphere of influence in Eastern Europe. Most Eastern European countries had communist governments installed by the USSR.
2) In 1949, the USSR exploded an atom bomb that it had developed during World War 2.
3) In 1947, US President Truman promised support to countries threatened by communist takeover — this became known as the 'Truman Doctrine'.
4) Truman also gave economic aid to Western European countries — hoping that this would help protect them from communist influence. This was called the Marshall Plan.
5) There was a crisis in Berlin in 1948-1949. The USSR, USA, France and Britain each had a zone they controlled in post-war Berlin. The USSR was angry when the other three decided to combine their zones. The USSR stopped supplies getting by land to West Berlin — so supplies had to be airlifted in (see p.21).

Events in the Far East made the Cold War worse

1) Communists came to power in China in 1949. They were led by Mao Tse-tung.
2) In 1950, communist North Korea invaded non-communist South Korea. The United Nations intervened to stop the communists taking over South Korea.
3) Once the UN forces had pushed them back past the original border, the communist Chinese sent an army to help the North.
4) The US General MacArthur, in charge of the UN forces, wanted to hit back at China itself. President Truman, afraid of starting World War 3, refused and insisted on a limited war.
5) In 1953 the Korean War ended with the pre-war border restored.

General MacArthur

Americans' Fear of Communism increased

1) American suspicions of the USSR grew — they thought it wanted world domination.
2) Under the 1947 Federal Employee Loyalty Program government employees were subjected to security checks. Their loyalty was questioned if they belonged to organisations with liberal ideas on race, disarmament or workers' rights.
3) Alger Hiss, a former senior member of the US State Department, was accused of spying and imprisoned for lying in court in 1950. This was an embarrassment to the US government.
4) By the 1950s, concerns about communism had started to cause a climate of fear and panic in the USA — this was called the Red Scare.

I spy — communists everywhere...

In the 1950s, there was huge fear and suspicion of communists in the USA. To understand why, you need to learn this stuff about the Cold War and what was going on in the world.

McCarthyism and the Red Scare

There was a 'Red Scare' in the 1950s — people were panicked by the communist threat.

The HUAC hunted for American Communists

1) The House Un-American Activities Committee (HUAC) was set up to investigate subversive activities. During the 1940s and 1950s it became focused on finding communists in the USA.
2) In 1947 HUAC began investigating the film industry, asking suspects at its hearings, "Are you now or have you ever been a member of the Communist Party?"
3) A group of directors and writers who refused to answer were blacklisted (meaning they would not be offered work in the industry again) and jailed. They became known as the Hollywood Ten. Hundreds more people were blacklisted in the following years.
4) Some famous actors like Humphrey Bogart supported the Hollywood Ten — but it didn't make any difference in the end. Some of those blacklisted went to Europe to find work.
5) Blacklisting also happened in broadcasting, schools and universities.

The FBI also investigated communists in America

J Edgar Hoover, director of the Federal Bureau of Investigation (FBI), was obsessed with "subversives". He kept thousands of secret dossiers on left-wing activists and thinkers, including six Nobel Prize-winning authors. The FBI conducted loyalty probes of millions of government employees.

McCarthy made Accusations with little evidence

1) In 1950, Senator McCarthy gave a speech during which he waved what he claimed was a list of 205 communists in the State Department (the US Foreign Office). He claimed some were giving information to the USSR — putting America at risk.
2) No one ever got a look at the list and many of the accusations were never proved. But newspapers published his allegations, and many people believed him.
3) McCarthy investigated possible communists. During Senate hearings he intimidated witnesses and pressured people to accuse others. He destroyed the careers of thousands of people.

McCarthy's activities were made possible by an already existing climate of fear. China had gone communist. The Russians had the bomb. And in 1951 two members of the US Communist Party, Julius and Ethel Rosenberg, were convicted of passing atomic secrets to the Russians. They were executed in 1953.

McCarthy Lost Popularity because of his Bullying Tactics

1) In 1953 McCarthy turned on the Army, accusing it of covering up communist infiltration. In the televised Army-McCarthy hearings in 1954, his bullying of witnesses turned public opinion against him. His Senate colleagues finally voted 67-22 to censure him in December 1954.
2) However, anti-communist feeling remained strong. The Communist Control Act in 1954 allowed dismissal from the civil service for political beliefs.

Red Scare — BOO!

The playwright Arthur Miller was blacklisted for refusing to give information to HUAC. He wrote a play called 'The Crucible' about a 17th century witch hunt — a symbol for McCarthyism.

Civil Rights Struggle in the 50s

In the 1940s and 1950s, African Americans were still denied the rights promised by the <u>American constitution</u>. Many states were still <u>segregated</u> (see p.67) and <u>racist attitudes</u> were common.

African Americans fought in World War 2

1) World War 2 started in 1939, but the <u>USA</u> didn't join the fighting until <u>December 1941</u>.
2) About a <u>million</u> African Americans fought in the American <u>armed forces</u> during the war.
3) The army was <u>segregated</u> — African Americans served in <u>separate military units</u> to whites.
4) African Americans saw action on <u>all fronts</u> and often distinguished themselves in the fighting, for example in the <u>Battle of the Bulge</u> in 1944 and at <u>Iwo Jima</u> in 1945.
5) However, because of racism, <u>no</u> African Americans were awarded the <u>Medal of Honor</u>.
6) Some <u>concessions</u> were made for the sake of <u>military efficiency</u>. African Americans were admitted to the <u>Marine Corps</u> for the first time. The first <u>African-American fighter pilots</u> flew combat missions.
7) African American soldiers fought for <u>freedom</u> abroad — but returned home to a society in which they were <u>oppressed</u> and <u>discriminated against</u>.
8) After the war, in <u>1948</u>, President Truman ended segregation in the <u>armed forces</u>.

African Americans remained Second-Class Citizens

In 1941, President Roosevelt had signed an executive order <u>banning racial discrimination</u> in <u>defence industries</u>. This caused <u>resentment</u> from some white workers. <u>Race riots</u> broke out in the industrial city of <u>Detroit</u> in 1943 — during which 25 African Americans and 9 white Americans were killed.

In the <u>South</u> of the USA, <u>segregation</u> was enforced by <u>law</u> in most aspects of <u>daily life</u> — schools, restaurants, theatres, workplaces, public transport and public toilets. Most white people thought this was <u>normal</u> and unremarkable. In the <u>North</u>, there was some <u>informal segregation</u> — reflecting and reinforcing African Americans' <u>lower social status</u>. Average wealth and living standards remained comparatively low for African Americans across the whole country.

The <u>Ku Klux Klan</u> (see p.67) was a <u>secret</u> organisation that believed in <u>white supremacy</u> — and used <u>violence</u> to intimidate African Americans. It had declined in popularity by the 1940s but was <u>still active</u> — and many people still shared its beliefs.

Civil Rights — in the land of the not yet free...

Despite gaining freedom from slavery after the civil war, African Americans were still <u>heavily oppressed</u> in the South. See page 67 for more on how prejudice was rife in pre-war America. Make sure you learn about the impact of World War 2, and how bad things remained at home.

Civil Rights Struggle in the 50s

With the help of the <u>Supreme Court</u>, the African Americans began to gain civil rights.

Justice lay in Enforcing the Constitution

The USA's <u>Declaration of Independence</u> and <u>Constitution</u> promise <u>all citizens</u> certain <u>rights</u>, including equal protection by the law. One strategy for gaining civil rights for African Americans was to appeal back to these <u>iconic American documents</u>. This approach, combined with <u>non-violent protest</u>, was pursued by <u>organisations</u> such as:

- The <u>NAACP</u> — National Association for the Advancement of Colored People — funded court cases challenging discrimination.
- The <u>SCLC</u> — Southern Christian Leadership Conference, founded in 1957 by Martin Luther King and Ralph Abernathy — used the churches' strength for protests.
- The <u>SNCC</u> — Student Nonviolent Coordinating Committee, formed in 1960.

The Supreme Court ruled against Segregated Education

1) Following campaigns by the NAACP, the <u>US Supreme Court</u> — which interprets the Constitution — ruled in the case <u>Brown v Board of Education of Topeka (1954)</u> that <u>racial segregation</u> in <u>state schools</u> was <u>unconstitutional</u>.
2) Since the <u>Constitution</u> is the <u>highest law</u> of the land, the federal (central) government was obliged to intervene when it was contradicted by <u>local state law</u>.
3) In 1957 President Eisenhower ordered 1000 paratroopers to the <u>Central High School</u> campus at <u>Little Rock</u>, Arkansas, to enforce the admission of <u>nine African-American pupils</u> in the face of local <u>mob violence</u>.
4) In both the above cases the <u>state governor</u>, backed by passionate <u>public support</u> from white people for segregation, did all he could to <u>defy</u> the federal authorities.

The Montgomery Bus Boycott — a victory for Integration

Rosa Parks

1) In 1955 in Montgomery, Alabama, <u>Rosa Parks</u> refused to give up her seat on the bus for a white man. She was <u>arrested</u>.
2) Black ministers, led by 26-year-old <u>Martin Luther King</u>, organised a <u>bus boycott</u> in protest. African Americans supported the boycott by walking to work or sharing cars for a year, until the Supreme Court finally ruled that Alabama's <u>bus segregation laws</u> were <u>unconstitutional</u>.
3) The <u>success</u> of this <u>peaceful protest</u> was inspirational to all who opposed segregation in the South.

The Civil Rights Acts of 1957 and 1960 were ineffective

1) The 1957 act created a <u>Civil Rights Commission</u> to investigate obstruction of <u>voting rights</u>.
2) The 1960 act increased <u>record-keeping</u> and supervision of <u>voting procedures</u>.
3) Neither act achieved much in practice, but a <u>small beginning</u> had been made by Congress.

All men are created equal...

... or so says the <u>Declaration of Independence</u> which, along with the <u>Constitution</u>, has a lot to say about <u>freedom</u> and <u>equality</u> — but African Americans still had to struggle to achieve theirs.

Civil Rights Movement in the 60s

Martin Luther King, the first president of the SCLC, was committed to non-violent struggle.

Non-Violent Protest won support

1) Martin Luther King and other activists used peaceful protests like marches, sit-ins and freedom rides (see box below) — gaining publicity and sympathy for the cause.
2) Many peaceful protests were undertaken by civil rights activists:

- In 1960, four African-American students started a series of sit-ins at segregated lunch counters at the Woolworths in Greensboro, North Carolina. These protests spread and some succeeded in forcing the desegregation of facilities.
- The Freedom Rides of 1961, organised by CORE (Congress of Racial Equality) and the SNCC, saw groups of African Americans and white Americans sitting together on bus trips into the South. Segregation on bus services had been ruled unconstitutional by the Supreme Court. There was a violent reaction to the Freedom Rides by some white people in the South.

The Birmingham victory convinced the President

1) President Kennedy (who came to power in 1961) at first gave limited support for African-American civil rights. He didn't want to alienate Southern white voters.
2) King and the SCLC organised protests in Birmingham, Alabama in April 1963. Protesters were met by police with fire hoses, truncheons and police dogs. Images of the harsh treatment of the protesters in the media gained support for their cause. King and hundreds of others were jailed. But in the end the Birmingham authorities gave way and agreed some concessions.
3) President Kennedy decided it was time to send a major Civil Rights Bill to Congress.

Next came Pressure on Congress

1) In August 1963, 250 000 demonstrators marched on Washington, where King spoke of his dream of a non-racist America.
2) But when Kennedy was assassinated in November 1963, his Civil Rights Bill had still not passed. He was replaced by President Johnson.
3) Despite the fact that Kennedy was from liberal Massachusetts in the North, and Johnson from segregated Texas in the South, it was Johnson who was more effective in achieving civil rights.

Martin Luther King

Important Acts were passed in 1964 and 1965

1) The Civil Rights Act of 1964 empowered the federal government to enforce desegregation in all public places. This was a big victory for the civil rights movement.
2) Voting rights were still a problem. In theory, African Americans could vote, but in the South all kinds of local rules were invented to stop them.
3) In the "Freedom Summer" of 1964 thousands of student volunteers spent vacations in Mississippi in a drive for voter registration. Three of these students were murdered.
4) In March 1965 the police in Selma, Alabama, used clubs and tear gas on civil rights marchers and again the brutality was televised. In response, King — who had been awarded the Nobel Peace Prize in 1964 — led a march through Alabama from Selma to Montgomery.
5) In August 1965 Johnson signed the Voting Rights Act. Federal registrars would now enforce voting rights. This was another major success for the civil rights movement.

Civil Rights — a victory for non-violence...

King was influenced by Gandhi who used non-violent civil disobedience against the British in India.

Civil Rights Movement in the 60s

The late 1960s and early 1970s saw the rise of a more <u>confrontational approach</u> to civil rights.

There was still Discrimination and Unrest

1) Formal civil rights <u>weren't enough</u> to help African Americans trapped in <u>poverty</u>.
2) The <u>Vietnam War</u> began to absorb funds which might otherwise have been available for more spending on <u>social programmes</u>.
3) Some African Americans became <u>impatient</u> with King's leadership and <u>non-violent</u> methods.
4) There were many inner-city <u>riots</u> by African Americans in the mid-1960s. 34 people were killed in a 6-day riot in the <u>Watts</u> district of Los Angeles in <u>August 1965</u>. The <u>8-day Detroit riot</u> of <u>July 1967</u> left 43 dead.

Martin Luther King was Assassinated in 1968

1) In <u>1966</u> Martin Luther King went north to <u>Chicago</u> to organise marches against discrimination in <u>housing</u> — a problem not dealt with by the 1964 Civil Rights Act.
2) The government gave no support because President Johnson was angered at the "<u>ingratitude</u>" of black leaders who had <u>criticised</u> his <u>Vietnam War policy</u>.
3) Congress did pass an effective Civil Rights Act for <u>housing</u> after King's <u>assassination</u> in April 1968 had triggered more riots in more than 100 <u>cities</u>.

Some groups favoured Violent Protest

Malcolm X <u>rejected</u> integration and non-violence. He called the peaceful march on Washington the "<u>farce on Washington</u>". His preaching drew converts to the African-American separatist organisation, the <u>Nation of Islam</u>. Malcolm X developed more 'inclusive' views and left the Nation of Islam in 1964. He was <u>killed</u> by Nation of Islam members in February <u>1965</u>.

In 1966 SNCC chairman Stokely Carmichael popularised the "<u>Black Power</u>" slogan. Under his leadership, the SNCC <u>expelled</u> its white members. In Newark in 1967, after a riot in which over 20 African Americans had been killed by police, a <u>Black Power</u> conference passed resolutions calling for a <u>separate African-American nation</u> and <u>militia</u>.

The <u>Black Panther Party</u> was founded in 1966 by <u>Huey P. Newton</u> and <u>Bobby Seale</u>. Its members wore uniforms and went on armed patrol, claiming to defend African Americans from police violence. They also carried out programmes providing free breakfasts for children, and <u>education</u> and <u>healthcare</u> for <u>African Americans</u>.

Affirmative Action gave African Americans opportunities

1) President Johnson sought to combat the under-representation of African Americans in many areas of <u>employment</u> with a <u>preferential hiring policy</u>.
2) Under President Nixon, people began to criticise this policy as "<u>reverse discrimination</u>".
3) However, from 1969 Nixon encouraged the growth of African American-owned businesses with the Small Business Administration's <u>set-aside programme</u>. This guaranteed that a proportion of government contracts would be awarded to ethnic minority owned firms.
4) During the 1970s attempts were made to integrate <u>schools</u> by "<u>busing</u>" children from different areas to make sure <u>schools</u> were ethnically mixed. It caused much <u>resistance</u> — many white Americans moved out to the suburbs or put their children in private schools to avoid it.

Martin Luther King's death shocked America...

King was <u>shot</u> on a hotel balcony — an escaped prisoner was later convicted of his <u>murder</u>.

Civil Rights of Hispanic Americans

African Americans weren't the only group in the USA who struggled against discrimination.

People emigrated from Latin America to the USA

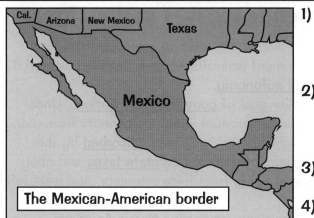

The Mexican-American border

1) The states bordering Mexico — Texas, New Mexico, Arizona and California — attracted much immigration from Mexico and other countries in Latin America.
2) To help the wartime labour shortage, from 1942 the Bracero Program allowed Mexican labourers to work temporarily in the US. The scheme lasted till 1964.
3) Millions more came as illegal immigrants — the 2000-mile border was difficult to police.
4) Mexican Americans faced segregation in schools, housing and employment.

The war sparked an era of Progress

1) Hundreds of thousands of Hispanic Americans served in the US armed forces in World War 2.
2) There was some racism against Hispanic Americans. In 1943 Los Angeles erupted in the Zoot Suit Riots — American sailors spent 10 days seeking out and beating up Latino teenagers.
3) After the war, the League of United Latin American Citizens and the American GI Forum mounted legal challenges to overturn school segregation in California and the exclusion of Mexican Americans from Texas juries.
4) In 1954 the Supreme Court in the case Hernandez v Texas declared that the 14th Amendment outlawing racial discrimination applied not just to African Americans but to all races.
5) Founded in 1968, the Mexican American Legal Defence and Educational Fund (MALDEF) became the most prominent Mexican-American civil rights organisation.

Cesar Chavez led the farm workers

1) Cesar Chavez, the grandson of Mexican immigrants, formed the United Farm Workers union in 1962. From 1965 he organised a 10-year campaign to improve the pay and working conditions of migrant workers, including a nationwide grape boycott in 1967.
2) In 1975 the Agricultural Labor Relations Act protected the right of farm workers to unionise. Chavez's success played a part in raising awareness of the wider struggle for Hispanic-American rights.

United Farm Workers' flag

The 1965 Immigration Act loosened restrictions

1) US immigration rules were based on a system of national quotas designed to reflect the existing ethnic structure of the USA. In the 1960s liberals denounced this as race bias.
2) The 1965 Immigration Act set preference categories based less on country of origin and more on kinship relations and occupation. Immigration from Latin America and Asia increased.

The Zoot Suit Riots — a fashion crime...

Zoot suits were oversized suits popular with Latin American teenagers in the 1940s. Some people said they wasted material — bad in wartime. But hardly justification for a riot...

Civil Rights of Native Americans

Native Americans suffered discrimination. Traditionally many tribes had led a nomadic lifestyle on the plains — but <u>white settlers</u> in the 19th century had forced them off much of the land.

Native American Land and Independence was under Threat

1) The <u>1934 Indian Reorganisation Act</u> had halted previous attempts to break up tribes and enforce assimilation. Now substantial self-government was offered to tribes who wanted it, in an effort to restore their <u>sovereignty</u> and <u>cultural autonomy</u>.

2) After World War 2, Congress reverted to the earlier goal of <u>complete assimilation</u>. Under this '<u>termination</u>' policy, started in the 1950s, the government withdrew benefits from many tribes. Many reservations (areas set aside for Native Americans) were <u>absorbed</u> by the states, becoming new counties. 'Terminated' tribes now had to pay <u>state taxes</u> and obey <u>state regulations</u>. Many had to sell <u>land</u> or <u>mineral rights</u> to outside interests, and were left <u>poorer than before</u>.

3) In the 1960s the Supreme Court began issuing decisions supporting <u>Native American sovereignty</u> and recognising the tribes' legal status as <u>higher</u> than that of the states, which limited the power of the states over the reservations.

AIM struggled for Native American Rights

1) The <u>American Indian Movement</u> (<u>AIM</u>) was formed in <u>1968</u> in response to police harassment in Minneapolis. It became a national organisation concerned also with issues such as <u>living standards</u> and <u>treaty rights</u>.

2) In <u>1972</u> AIM members joined with seven other organisations in the <u>Trail of Broken Treaties</u>, a march on Washington. The protesters vandalised the headquarters of the <u>Bureau of Indian Affairs</u> (<u>BIA</u>) — the federal agency which <u>manages</u> the <u>reservation system</u>.

3) Civil disobedience '<u>fish-ins</u>' brought success in the <u>1974 Boldt Decision</u> in favour of Native American <u>fishing</u> and <u>hunting rights</u>.

4) By <u>1980</u> Native Americans had succeeded in forcing the government to <u>return</u> some important tribal lands and to provide <u>compensation</u> for some confiscated lands.

5) The <u>1978 Indian Religious Freedom Act</u> guaranteed protection for forms of <u>religious worship</u> and <u>access</u> to <u>sacred sites</u>.

There was conflict at Wounded Knee in 1973

1) A faction at the <u>Oglala Sioux reservation</u>, opposed to <u>corruption</u> in the way the reservation was managed, invited AIM to join a protest.

2) The protesters <u>seized</u> the village of <u>Wounded Knee</u> at <u>gunpoint</u>. Soon they were surrounded by a <u>military cordon</u>. The siege lasted for <u>71 days</u>. Shots were exchanged and two people were killed.

3) The <u>symbolism</u> of the site — scene of an 1890 <u>massacre</u> of Sioux by the Army — ensured national media attention.

4) Eventually, after a <u>negotiated settlement</u> of the local issues, the siege ended in a <u>triumph</u> for AIM.

Russell Means — one of AIM's leaders in the '70s

Native American Rights — AIM to learn the whole page...

Wounded Knee is a place with very <u>heavy significance</u> in Native American history. The 1890 massacre of Sioux is generally regarded as the <u>final event</u> in the Native American struggle against the expanding USA. So the siege there in <u>1973</u> made people sit up and take notice.

Women's Rights

The feminist movement gained momentum in the 1960s — and won better rights for women.

Women began to challenge Discrimination at Work

1) In 1960 women usually worked in low-paid jobs such as nursing, teaching, and clerical and domestic work. During the 1960s, women made up around 33-43 per cent of the total workforce, but their average earnings remained around 60 per cent that of men.
2) Eleanor Roosevelt pressured President Kennedy into creating a Presidential Commission on the Status of Women (1961) with herself as its head.
3) The 1963 Equal Pay Act made it illegal to pay women less than men for the same job. But the Equal Employment Opportunity Commission was understaffed and there was little to stop employers giving different job titles to men and women doing the same activities.
4) Title VII of the 1964 Civil Rights Act prohibited discrimination in employment on the basis of sex. But enforcement was slow to follow.
5) Available from 1960, the contraceptive pill ('the Pill') made it easier for women to postpone having children while they started a career.

Eleanor Roosevelt

The campaign group NOW was formed in 1966

1) Betty Friedan in 'The Feminine Mystique' (1963) criticised the isolation of women in the household — saying many felt trapped in the homemaker role.
2) Friedan was one of the founders of the National Organisation for Women (NOW) — founded in 1966 to campaign for women's legal, educational and professional equality.
3) NOW pressured Congressmen into passing the Equal Rights Amendment (ERA) in 1972 — but the Amendment failed to achieve ratification by the necessary three-quarters of states.
4) Opposition to the ratification of the ERA included women who wanted a return to "traditional" femininity. Conservative activist Phyllis Schlafly organised a group called "Stop ERA".
5) However, the objectives of ERA were largely achieved by other means — especially a more vigorous enforcement of Title VII of the 1964 Civil Rights Act.
6) Title IX of the Educational Amendments Act (1972) forced government-funded educational establishments to provide equal facilities and opportunities for both sexes.

Feminists began to campaign against the objectification of women. Feminists protested at the 1968 Miss America beauty pageant — they crowned a sheep their own 'Miss America'.

The right to Abortion was a Controversial Issue

Feminists argued that women had the right to choose abortion. The Supreme Court ruled in the case Roe v Wade (1973) that state laws banning abortion were unconstitutional. But in response to pressure from religious groups, Congress passed the Hyde Amendment in 1976. This stopped Medicaid (the medical assistance programme for the poor) from funding abortions.

Women's liberation — get learning NOW...

The women's movement achieved a lot for women — including basic rights we take for granted nowadays like equal pay and equal educational opportunities.

Revision Summary

It's another glorious revision summary. It's the usual drill — answer all the questions, then see what you got wrong and revise any weak spots. You'll be an old hand at it by now.

1) What was the Marshall Plan?

2) What was the name of the American general in charge of UN forces in the Korean War?

3) What was the 'Red Scare' in the 1950s?

4) What was the 'Hollywood Ten'?

5) Who was the director of the FBI during the Red Scare?

6) Why did Senator McCarthy lose popularity?

7) What was segregation?

8) What does SCLC stand for?

9) What was the ruling in the case Brown v Board of Education of Topeka (1954)?

10) What act of resistance did Rosa Parks make to segregation in 1955?

11) Who spoke of his dream at a major 1963 civil rights march?

12) Who was murdered during the 'Freedom Summer'?

13) When was Martin Luther King assassinated?

14) How did Malcolm X's approach differ from Martin Luther King's?

15) Why was President Johnson's preferential hiring policy criticised?

16) What were the Zoot Suit Riots?

17) Who founded the United Farm Workers union in 1962?

18) What does AIM stand for?

19) Describe the events at Wounded Knee in 1973.

20) What Act made it illegal to pay women less than men for the same job?

21) What was the name of Betty Friedan's famous 1963 book?

22) What was the ruling about abortion in the case Roe v Wade (1973)?

The Need for Reform

In the 1890s many people in Britain weren't just poor, they were desperate.
There was no government help for the old, ill or unemployed.

Poor People faced serious hardship in the 1890s

1) The main help available for very poor people was the workhouses run by local councils.
They provided basic food and lodging in exchange for long hours in brutal conditions.
Many people saw going to the workhouse as shameful.

2) There was serious unemployment in some industries, and no 'dole' or unemployment benefit.

3) Old people who had no savings or family suffered very badly — there were no government
pensions. The only option for many old people was the workhouse.

4) Housing in poor areas was damp, cold and didn't have proper sewage systems. It was easy
to get ill in these conditions, which meant missing work, and maybe losing your job.

5) Many people couldn't afford doctors or medicine.

6) Many children had to go to work from an early age, and so missed getting an education.

7) Large numbers of people couldn't even afford to eat properly. Out of all the men recruited to
fight in the Boer War (1899-1902), half were malnourished.

Two reports said a Third of British people were Poor

Not everybody believed that poverty was all that bad — especially rich people.
Two reports said that poverty was serious, and that it affected large numbers of people.

Charles Booth published the first edition of Life and Labour of the People in 1889.
This showed that 30% of people in London were living in severe poverty, and that it was
sometimes impossible for people to find work, however hard they tried. He also showed that
wages for some jobs were so low that they weren't enough to support a family.

Seebohm Rowntree had a factory in York. He didn't believe the problem was as
bad there as in London — so he did a survey of living conditions. The report of
his findings, Poverty, a Study of Town Life (published 1901) showed that 28% of
people in York were so poor that they couldn't afford basic food and housing.

Public Opinion on helping poor people began to Change

There was no way you could put a third of the population into the workhouse. Britain needed
a new approach to deal with poverty. Many people had an opinion on how it should be done.

1) Popular and well-respected writers like George Bernard Shaw, J. Galsworthy, Charles Dickens
and H. G. Wells wrote about how poor people lived. They said the poor needed help, and the
government should pass laws to make sure it happened.

2) People involved in public health and medicine said the government should get more involved
in health issues.

3) Socialists argued that wealth should be more equally spread between working people and
people like factory owners and land owners, who were traditionally the richest.

4) The Labour Party was the only mainstream socialist political party. They argued that the
government should give financial help to the poorest members of society. Labour was
attracting more and more working-class supporters.

Rowntree — social reformer AND inventor of Fruit Gums...

Learn the examples of the problems facing poor people, the two reports, and the new
ideas on helping the poor. Scribble them down, and check you've got them right.

Conservatives, Liberals and Labour

Pressure was growing for the government to deal with poverty. The main parties — the Liberals and Conservatives — traditionally felt it wasn't the government's role. But things were changing.

The political parties had Different Attitudes to Poverty

The oldest, most powerful political parties — the Liberals and the Conservatives — didn't really agree with giving government help to people. They believed that:
1) the government should interfere as little as possible in people's lives
2) it was wrong to raise taxes as people should decide how to spend their own money
3) giving poor people money was morally wrong as it undermined their independence.

The Labour Party didn't have many MPs before 1906, but they did have growing support from working people. They believed that:
1) the poorest people in society should get government help
2) the government should get the cash to pay for this from taxes
3) the government should also take over (nationalise) the major industries and make use of the profits.

Some Liberals and some Conservatives were more open to the idea of the government helping the poor — especially if it helped their party win votes from Labour.

A Royal Commission investigated Poverty

In 1905 the Conservative government set up a Royal Commission to look at the Poor Law. This was the 19th-century law which set up the workhouses and other help for the poor. The Commission was supposed to decide whether the help given by the Poor Law was good enough. But the members of the Commission couldn't agree about what caused poverty so they published two reports:

The Majority Report (what the majority of the commission thought)
- If people were poor it was their own fault.
- They made themselves poor by gambling and drinking — so they didn't deserve help.
- Enough was being done for the poor already.

The Minority Report (what the minority of the commission thought)
- People couldn't help being poor.
- Illness, old age and a shortage of jobs made people poor.
- They thought more should be done to prevent people being poor.

After 1906 the Liberals brought in Social Reforms

1) In 1906 the Liberal Party won a landslide general election victory over the Conservatives.
2) 29 Labour Party MPs were elected — giving them a good position to push for help for the poor.
3) The Minority Report, the success of the Labour Party and pressure from the general public all encouraged the Liberals to bring in laws to deal with poverty.
4) The Liberals had to compete with Labour for the support of working-class voters — this led to the emergence of "New Liberalism" which favoured government intervention to help the poor.
5) The poor physical condition of volunteers for the Boer War had been a shock. If Britain was involved in a major war, it would need a healthy working class to fight as soldiers.
6) David Lloyd George and Winston Churchill* were the MPs who worked hardest to drive the bills through. They wanted to help the poor, but were also keen to make a name for themselves.

*Watch out for Churchill — he was a Liberal until the 1920s, when he became a Conservative.

David Lloyd George — so good they named him thrice...

We're used to the idea of benefits and pensions being paid by the government but at the time this was a new idea. Scribble down the reasons why the Liberals brought in social reforms after 1906.

Laws to Help Children and Old People

The Liberals <u>didn't plan</u> to help <u>everyone</u> — just the people with the <u>worst problems</u> — children from poor families, old people, ill people, and people who were out of work or badly paid. Unfortunately they've left you <u>reams of laws</u> to learn...

Children needed Special Protection

In <u>1906</u> the <u>School Meals Act</u> allowed <u>LEAs</u> to supply <u>free</u> school meals paid for out of <u>rates</u>.

<u>LEAs</u> = Local Education Authorities. They were in charge of running state schools.
<u>rates</u> = local council tax

In <u>1907</u> LEAs started giving children at their schools <u>free medical inspections</u>. Many of them built clinics where they could hold the inspections. Poor children also got <u>free medical treatment</u>.

In <u>1908</u> Parliament passed the <u>Children and Young Persons' Act</u> (also known as the <u>Children's Charter</u>) to give children some legal protection. The Charter made it illegal for children younger than <u>16</u> to <u>buy cigarettes</u>, <u>go into a pub</u> or <u>beg</u>. It also set up special <u>juvenile courts</u> — so <u>young offenders</u> wouldn't be <u>tried</u> in an <u>adult court</u>.

I think it was the sprouts.

<u>Herbert Samuel</u> from the Home Office tried to help <u>young offenders</u>:

1) He set up special prisons, known as <u>borstals</u>, for young offenders — so they wouldn't have to go to adult prisons.
2) He set up the <u>probation service</u> to try to keep young people from reoffending.

Elderly people got State Pensions

In <u>1908</u> <u>David Lloyd George</u> was Chancellor of the Exchequer. He introduced the <u>Old Age Pensions Act</u>. These are the most important bits of the Act:

1) The pension was for people <u>over 70</u> on low incomes.
2) The scheme was <u>non-contributory</u> — you didn't have to pay money in to get a pension when you retired. The pensions were paid for by money raised through <u>ordinary taxes</u>.
3) In the <u>1908</u> budget £1 200 000 of tax money was set aside to pay for pensions.
4) Single people with an income of <u>less than £21 per year</u> got 5 shillings per week. <u>Married couples</u> with an income of <u>less than £21 per year</u> got 7s 6d (7 shillings & 6 pence) per week.
5) Anyone whose income was <u>between £21 and £31 per year</u> got a smaller pension.
6) People with an income of <u>over</u> £31 per year didn't get a pension at all.
7) The first pensions were paid on <u>1 January 1909</u>.

Although Labour said 5 shillings was <u>too little</u>, the pension was <u>immensely popular</u>. Lloyd George took the <u>credit</u>.

We are lifting the shadow of the workhouse from the homes of the poor.

Remember the aim <u>wasn't</u> to help everyone, just the <u>poorest people</u>.

David Lloyd George

The Old Age Pensions Act — an over-70s free-for-all...

Children got <u>legal protection</u>, <u>school dinners</u>, <u>medical check-ups</u> and <u>borstal</u>. Old people got pensions. Make sure you know the dates and names of the Acts.

Laws Protecting Working People

The Liberals also passed laws to help <u>working people</u>. Get all of these <u>clear</u> in your mind now — you need to know the <u>name</u> and <u>date</u> of each Act, and <u>what it did</u> to help people.

The National Insurance Act of 1911

In <u>1911</u> Lloyd George introduced the <u>National Insurance Act</u>. Lloyd George got a lot of the ideas for this Act from a <u>similar scheme</u> running in <u>Germany</u>.

> The Act came in two parts. Part One's covered here. Part Two's covered on the next page.

Part One helped with Health Insurance

Part One was to help workers pay for <u>health insurance</u>. The insurance was to pay for <u>treatment</u> and provide <u>sick pay</u> when people were too ill to work. The National Insurance Act said the government would <u>top up</u> the money that workers paid into insurance schemes.

1) The Act covered workers earning <u>less than £160 per year</u>.
2) <u>Each week</u> workers paid <u>4 old pence</u> out of their wages into a <u>central fund</u>. Employers added <u>3 old pence</u> per week and the government added another <u>2 old pence</u> per week.
3) Sick pay of up to <u>10 shillings per week</u> was paid to <u>male</u> workers if they were off work ill for more than <u>four days</u>. This sick pay would be paid for several months. The worker was also entitled to <u>medical attention</u>.

> 4) Women <u>didn't pay as much</u> in or <u>get as much</u> out, because they <u>didn't earn as much</u> in the first place.
> 5) Women were paid <u>7s 6d</u> a week <u>sick pay</u>. They also got a one-off <u>maternity grant</u> of <u>30 shillings</u>.

6) <u>Names</u> of workers on the National Insurance scheme were put on a special list known as a <u>doctors' 'panel'</u>. Doctors were <u>paid</u> a sum by the government for every patient on the panel.
7) The scheme was organised through organisations approved by the government — <u>friendly</u> <u>societies</u>, <u>trade unions</u> and <u>private insurance companies</u>.
8) The scheme caused <u>controversy</u> — Conservatives said the government had <u>no right</u> to force people to contribute from their wages, and many socialists said there should be <u>higher</u> <u>taxes on rich people</u> to pay for it instead of workers having to contribute. But it was still <u>passed</u>.

> friendly society = a kind of voluntary society in which members paid a subscription in exchange for financial and medical help if they became sick.

> Workers are getting nine pence for four pence.

David Lloyd George

> <u>Ten million workers</u> now had health insurance.

I can't wait to find out what happens in part two...

These laws were to help some of the <u>poorest</u> people in the country. Remember that Britain was a lot more <u>industrial</u> at the time, so there were more <u>accidents</u> and <u>industrial illnesses</u>.

Laws Protecting Working People

Here's Part Two of the National Insurance Act, and a couple of other Liberal laws to help workers.

Part Two set up Unemployment Benefit for a few trades

Part Two of the National Insurance Act provided unemployment benefit for workers in shipbuilding, iron founding and construction. These were industries where workers were quite regularly out of work for several weeks at a time.

...iron foundries and construction...

Shipbuilding...

...but once again nobody's remembered the witches.

Annual General Witchfest 1911

It was a contributory scheme. Employers and employees each paid 2½d per week into an unemployment fund and the government paid 1¾d.

In return workers were paid 7 shillings per week for up to 15 weeks in any one year if they were unemployed. Payment started from the second week of unemployment.

The Trade Boards Act of 1909 set a Minimum Wage

Winston Churchill and William Beveridge put together the Trade Boards Act in 1909 to help sweated industry workers.

Sweated industries included tailoring, lace-making and cardboard-box making. The workers were often women or foreign immigrants who worked from home doing long hours for low wages.

> 1) The Act set up trade boards for each of the 'sweated industries'.
> 2) Every board was made up of equal numbers of workers and employers, and a neutral chairman.
> 3) The board's job was to decide a minimum wage for the industry.
> 4) Employers paying less than their trade board laid down could be fined.
> 5) Factory inspectors made sure the Act was put into practice.

By 1914 half a million workers were covered by the trade boards and so had the security of a minimum wage.

The Labour Exchanges Act set up Job Centres

Churchill and Beveridge also worked together on the Labour Exchanges Act. This was passed in 1909 too.

> 1) Labour exchanges were like job centres. Unemployed workers could go there to find out about job vacancies.
> 2) Within five years there was a network right across Britain.
> 3) One million jobs a year were filled through the exchanges.

The Labour Exchange Act — perfect for swapping jobs...

There's a lot of nasty fiddly detail here — don't panic if you can't remember it all. The easiest way to learn the important bits is by making a timeline of Acts and dates. Then make sure you can scribble down the main point of each Act — who it was meant to help, and what they got.

Effects of the Liberal Reforms

The Liberals' reforms wouldn't do much good if they couldn't <u>pay</u> for them. They had to get the money through <u>taxes</u> — one reason why some people <u>didn't</u> welcome the reforms with <u>open arms</u>.

Lloyd George wanted to Raise Taxes to pay for reforms

In <u>1909</u> the Liberal Chancellor of the Exchequer Lloyd George decided he'd have to <u>raise taxes</u> to pay for the reforms. He proposed the tax increases in the <u>1909</u> budget. It was designed to tax the rich <u>more heavily</u> than the poor — so it became known as <u>the People's Budget</u>.

- <u>Income tax</u> would go up from 5 pence to 6 pence in the pound.
- There'd be a new <u>super tax</u> of 1s. 2d. in the pound on incomes <u>over £3000</u> per year.
- The inheritance tax — called <u>death duties</u> — would go up.
- Tax on <u>tobacco</u> and <u>spirits</u> would go up.

The Liberals had to call a General Election in 1910

To become <u>law</u> the Budget had to be passed by the House of Commons <u>and</u> the House of Lords.

1) Although <u>the Conservatives</u> were <u>opposed</u> to the Budget, the bill got through the <u>Commons</u>. But it was <u>rejected</u> in the House of <u>Lords</u> where Conservatives held the majority.
2) The Liberals <u>couldn't</u> see any way of getting the bill through Parliament. This was a constitutional crisis — the <u>unelected</u> House of Lords was <u>blocking</u> the will of the <u>elected</u> House of Commons.
3) The Liberals called a <u>general election</u> to make sure they had the British people's support. The <u>only issue</u> of the campaign was the People's Budget.
4) The <u>Liberal Party won</u> the election. They reintroduced the Budget and finally it was passed by the <u>Commons and the Lords</u>.

To prevent such crises the <u>Parliament Act</u> was passed in <u>1911</u>. The Lords were <u>no longer</u> allowed to reject <u>bills on financial issues</u>. They could reject other bills <u>twice</u>.

The Liberal Reforms left some problems Unsolved...

1) Hardly any of the new schemes were designed to help the <u>whole population</u>.
2) The <u>National Insurance Act</u> Part One <u>didn't</u> cover the worker's <u>family</u>. Part <u>Two</u> only covered a <u>few</u> industries.
3) The reforms <u>didn't</u> replace the old Poor Law. <u>Workhouses</u> weren't abolished until 1930.

...but Changed Attitudes to helping the poor

1) This was the first time that <u>national taxes</u> had been used to help the poor.
2) The state took on <u>responsibility</u> for protecting citizens from <u>extreme hardship</u> in sickness, old age and unemployment for the <u>first time</u>.
3) The schemes were introduced <u>all across the country</u> — they weren't just local affairs.
4) <u>Large numbers</u> of people were covered by some of the schemes — the National Insurance Act Part One covered 10 million workers.
5) The new provisions <u>didn't</u> have the same <u>stigma</u> as the workhouse and because of the new laws fewer people had to rely on the Poor Law system.
6) The number of <u>non-government</u> welfare organisations, e.g. friendly societies, schemes run by churches etc, <u>declined</u>.

"The People" 1 — "Peers of the Realm" 0...

The fact that the Liberals had to call a <u>general election</u> and <u>change the law</u> about the House of Lords shows what a <u>stir</u> they'd caused. The way they <u>changed attitudes</u> is really important too.

Women's Rights in 1900

Women in the <u>1890s</u> were treated differently from men. Most women didn't go to school or university, and instead spent their lives raising <u>children</u> and working to <u>run a house</u>.

Women's legal rights Weren't Equal — but Getting Better

For a long time married women were <u>not protected</u> in law — but several new laws in the 19th century gave them more <u>rights in marriage</u>.

<u>1857</u> The Matrimonial Clauses Act made it easier for a woman to get a <u>divorce</u> through ordinary law courts. You had to prove your husband had committed <u>adultery</u> and another offence such as <u>cruelty</u> or <u>desertion</u> (leaving you). Before the Act, only <u>Parliament</u> could grant divorces.

<u>1870</u> The Married Women's Property Act gave women the right to <u>keep</u> their <u>earnings</u> when they got married. Before the Act it <u>all</u> went to the <u>husband</u> automatically. In <u>1882</u>, a second <u>Married Women's Property Act</u> gave married women the right to keep their <u>property</u> as well.

<u>1886</u> The Married Women (Maintenance in Case of Desertion) Act said that a husband who left his wife had to keep <u>paying</u> for her maintenance — i.e. her <u>living expenses</u>.
The Guardianship of Children Act allowed women to be their children's <u>legal guardians</u> if the father died or if the marriage broke up. Being the <u>legal guardian</u> meant having <u>responsibility</u> for any property left to the children as well as seeing they were properly looked after.

Some Professions were Open to Women

Florence Nightingale

1) Many working-class women had <u>jobs</u> as well as running the home, e.g. in the <u>textile industry</u>. These jobs tended to be <u>low paid</u> with <u>poor conditions</u>.
2) Middle-class women were less likely to work outside the home. Access to <u>higher education</u> and <u>professional jobs</u> was <u>limited</u>.
3) <u>Queen's College, London</u> was opened to train women <u>teachers</u> in <u>1848</u>.
4) <u>Florence Nightingale</u> established <u>nursing</u> as a respectable job. She set up a <u>training school</u> where women could train to become nurses.

Women Couldn't Vote in national elections

During the 19th century, several <u>reform acts</u> had given more people in Britain the <u>vote</u> — but only men. Most people thought it was <u>perfectly sensible</u> that women <u>didn't</u> have the vote.

1) They thought the <u>public sphere</u> was for <u>men</u>. <u>Women</u> should look after the <u>home</u>.
2) Many people believed that women weren't very <u>rational</u> and so couldn't make <u>big decisions</u>.
3) Many politicians thought that men needed to be <u>householders</u> to get the vote. Only a very few rich women <u>owned</u> houses or <u>paid the rent</u>, so it would be a bit odd to give them a vote.
4) If only rich women got the vote they'd probably <u>vote Conservative</u>. The Liberals didn't like that idea.

After <u>1894</u> married women were allowed to <u>vote</u> for <u>district councils</u>, and to sit on the councils. But they still <u>couldn't vote</u> in national elections for MPs or <u>become MPs</u> themselves. Campaigners for votes for women argued that:

1) Women's rights and opportunities were <u>improving</u> — being given the vote was a <u>natural step forward</u>.
2) Women were just as <u>capable</u> as men of making <u>sound decisions</u>.
3) Women had gained the <u>vote</u> in some other countries, e.g. in <u>New Zealand</u> in 1893.

You've got to fight for your right — to vote in local elections...

Learn <u>why</u> people thought women <u>shouldn't vote</u>, and the <u>four Acts</u> which gave women <u>more legal rights</u>.

The Campaign for the Vote 1900-1914

There had been campaigns for women's votes before 1900, but the campaigns from 1900 to 1914 were more energetic than ever. Some campaigns were peaceful, some weren't...

The Suffragists were Moderate in their protests

1) The suffragists' formal name was the NATIONAL UNION OF WOMEN'S SUFFRAGE SOCIETIES (NUWSS).
2) They were founded in 1897. Their leader was Millicent Fawcett.
3) Their main tactics were persuasion, meetings and petitions to Parliament.

suffrage = the right to vote

The Suffragettes were more Direct

1) The suffragettes' formal name was the WOMEN'S SOCIAL AND POLITICAL UNION (WSPU).
2) They were founded by Emmeline Pankhurst in 1903, with her daughters Christabel and Sylvia. Emmeline Pankhurst had previously campaigned to get women the vote in local elections.
3) The suffragettes thought the suffragists took things too slowly. They wanted results fast.
4) The suffragettes didn't mind getting arrested. It attracted some sympathy and showed they were serious. In 1905 Christabel Pankhurst and Annie Kenney ended up in prison for a week for heckling Sir Edward Grey, who was speaking at a meeting in Manchester.
5) They hoped the Liberal government after 1906 would be sympathetic. They were encouraged by the 1907 Qualification of Women Act which let women become county and borough councillors, or mayors. However, in 1908, Asquith, a Liberal, became Prime Minister — he was against votes for women.

After 1912 the protests got More Extreme

By 1912 the Liberal government had accepted the idea of some women voting, and tried to put it into their Plural Voting Bill for Parliament to discuss. But the Speaker refused to let them add it. The suffragettes were furious and protests got far more extreme and violent.

1) Suffragettes chained themselves to railings outside Downing Street and Buckingham Palace.
2) They physically assaulted politicians. The Prime Minister, Asquith, was attacked on a golf course. Suffragettes tried to tear off his clothes, and beat him with dog whips.
3) They destroyed paintings in the National Gallery, and smashed shop windows.
4) Suffragettes made arson attacks on post boxes, churches and railway stations. In 1913, they even bombed the house of Lloyd George, who was fairly sympathetic to votes for women.
5) At the 1913 Derby at Epsom, a suffragette called Emily Davison threw herself under the feet of the King's horse. She died of her injuries.

Suffragists thought these tactics held the campaign back. The government didn't want to be seen to be giving in to violence. The violence also put off many moderate supporters.

The Government dealt with the protests Harshly

1) They sent many suffragettes to prison. The suffragettes often went on hunger strike, so the prison authorities force-fed them, but this was dangerous and violent.
2) The so-called "Cat and Mouse" Act was passed in 1913. Under this Act the authorities could release hunger strikers then rearrest them when they were fit again.

Women's suffrage — I get the -gist...

Try not to get suffragettes and suffragists mixed up. Women didn't get the vote until after the First World War had changed things — there's more on this on p.113.

The War at Home

When the First World War broke out the government had to be sure Britain was <u>ready</u> to cope. They gave themselves <u>special powers</u> by...surprise... getting Parliament to pass a <u>law</u>.

Parliament passed the Defence of the Realm Act

The <u>Defence of the Realm Act</u> (DORA) was passed in <u>August 1914</u>, right at the start of the war. There were <u>two</u> basic things the government was trying to do:

1) Make sure the country had <u>enough resources</u> to fight the war.
2) Make sure <u>British people</u> were in a <u>fit state</u> to fight and support the war effort.

The law <u>allowed</u> the government to...

- take control of <u>vital industries</u> like coal mining
- take over <u>2.5 million acres of land</u> and <u>buildings</u>
- bring in <u>British Summer Time</u> for more daylight (working) hours
- control <u>drinking hours</u> and the <u>strength of alcohol</u>

- introduce <u>conscription</u>

- <u>stop people talking</u> about the war or spreading rumours
- <u>censor</u> newspapers
- enforce <u>rationing</u>

Thousands Volunteered to fight — but it Wasn't Enough

1) When war broke out, thousands of men <u>rushed</u> to volunteer for the fighting. They believed the war would be over <u>quickly</u> — 'by Christmas'. They thought it was going to be an <u>adventure</u>, and wanted to be <u>part of it</u>. The enthusiasm <u>didn't last</u>.

2) Kitchener, the Secretary for War, wanted to introduce conscription in 1914, but Asquith, the Prime Minister, refused. Instead, there was a massive poster campaign — the "Your Country Needs You" one.

3) By <u>1915</u> the number of <u>casualties</u> was going <u>up</u> — and the number of <u>volunteers</u> was slowing <u>down</u>. On the <u>Western Front</u> so many men were being killed and wounded that there <u>weren't enough</u> volunteers to <u>replace</u> them.

4) There was also a growing feeling that it <u>wasn't fair</u> that some men were <u>avoiding</u> military duty.

The Government introduced Conscription in 1916

1) All <u>single men</u> aged between <u>18 and 40</u> had to fight.
2) When there <u>still</u> weren't enough soldiers <u>married men</u> had to join up too.
3) People who didn't <u>believe</u> in fighting were called <u>conscientious objectors</u>. They were treated as <u>criminals</u> and sent to <u>prison</u>. They were seen as <u>traitors</u> because they refused to fight. Some were members of groups like the Quakers, who had <u>religious objections</u> to fighting. Many agreed to carry out non-violent war work, such as driving ambulances.

Women started doing "men's jobs"

I wonder what he's doing now...

Many of the <u>original volunteers</u> came from <u>heavy industries</u> like coal mining. There was a <u>shortage</u> of workers in these industries and without them Britain couldn't <u>supply the army</u>. When <u>conscription</u> started there were even <u>fewer men</u> available to do the <u>vital jobs</u>. <u>Women</u> started taking their places in the <u>pits</u> and <u>factories</u>.

I wonder what she's doing now...

Surviving at home — major changes were needed...

You've <u>got</u> to know all about the <u>Defence of the Realm Act</u>, and <u>conscription</u> — scribble and learn.

Food Shortages

Britain had problems keeping <u>food supplies</u> going in the war. Something needed to be done to make sure nobody starved. The important thing is to learn <u>all three</u> of Lloyd George's tactics.

German U-boats *made it hard to Import Food*

1) In <u>1914</u> Britain was used to <u>importing</u> quite a lot of food from the <u>United States</u> and countries that were part of the <u>Empire</u>.
2) Germany used <u>U-boats</u> (submarines) to <u>attack shipping</u> all round Britain and made it <u>impossible</u> to import all the food Britain needed to survive.
3) By <u>April 1917</u> Britain only had <u>six weeks'</u> supply of wheat. The Prime Minister, David Lloyd George, took <u>three big steps</u> to solve the food crisis:

1) Navy Convoys *protected Merchant Ships*

| BEFORE CONVOY SYSTEM | AFTER CONVOY SYSTEM |

Rats!

Ships travelling <u>alone</u> were <u>easy targets</u> for the U-boats. <u>25%</u> of merchant ships coming into Britain were being <u>sunk</u>.

The Navy began a <u>convoy system</u>. Merchant ships travelled in <u>groups</u> with an escort of <u>Royal Navy</u> ships to protect them.

U-boats <u>couldn't attack</u> as easily. With the convoy system <u>less than 1%</u> of ships were sunk.

2) Compulsory Rationing *started in 1918*

When food rationing started in <u>1917</u> it was <u>voluntary</u>. In <u>1918</u> shortages were still a problem and rationing was made <u>compulsory</u> for <u>beer, butter, sugar</u> and <u>meat</u>.

1) Everyone got <u>rationing coupons</u>. They had to <u>hand them over</u> when they bought <u>beer, butter, sugar</u> and <u>meat</u>. When the week's coupons for, say, <u>sugar</u>, ran out, they couldn't buy any more that week.
2) Some people <u>hoarded</u> food, partly because they were afraid it would <u>run out</u>, and partly because of <u>increasing prices</u>. They would sell it on <u>later</u>, creating a '<u>black market</u>' in food.
3) There were <u>shortages</u> of some kinds of food but <u>no-one</u> starved.
4) The government had never been <u>this involved</u> in organising people's daily lives before.

3) Britain Grew *more food*

1) Farmers were encouraged to use <u>more</u> of their land so they could <u>grow more food</u>.
2) The <u>Women's Land Army</u> was set up in 1917. Women from the Land Army were a <u>big</u> new labour force available to work on the <u>farms</u>.

Food supply — crucial to avoiding a crisis...

How Lloyd George <u>avoided</u> a <u>food supply crisis</u> isn't the most exciting topic in this section — but you've definitely got to know about the three steps he took: <u>convoys</u>, <u>rationing</u> and <u>production</u>.

Attitudes to the War in Britain

There's a dramatic difference between people's cheerful attitude at the beginning of the war and their horror at the waste of life by the end. Make sure you know why attitudes changed so much.

At the Start the war looked like an Adventure

In 1914 there was huge enthusiasm for the war. It seems strange now, but nobody at the time knew what it was going to be like. These are some of the things people felt about the war:

Fighting in the war would be an adventure.	It was right to fight for your country when it went to war.	The war would be "over by Christmas". Britain would win easily.

Obviously not everybody thought exactly like this — but a fair few did.

At first people Didn't Really Know what was going on

The government deliberately kept people ignorant of what was going on:

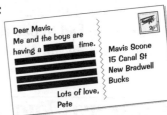

1) Letters from soldiers were censored.
2) Reporters weren't allowed to see battles very often.
3) Newspapers were censored from 1914.
4) No photographs could be taken which showed dead soldiers.
5) Casualty figures weren't available from the government.

Britain had never before been involved in a war where most of the fighting was done in trenches, or one in which so many people were killed. People away from the front couldn't imagine how terrible the war was.

During the war ordinary people's Attitudes Changed

The government couldn't keep the facts about the war secret for ever.
As the war carried on people couldn't help finding out more, and attitudes began to change.

1) During the war 1500 civilians were killed in bombing raids. This was a new and terrible danger.
2) There were no obvious successes on the Western Front up until 1918.
3) The government could hide the overall casualty figures, but they couldn't hide crippled and blinded veterans who returned to Britain, or keep deaths secret from the families of soldiers.
4) Rationing was difficult, and richer people felt it was a hardship. Taxes had increased to pay for the war. By 1917 most people in Britain were sick of the war, and wanted to see it end.

Britain used Propaganda to encourage people to fight

1) Propaganda posters were used to encourage men to sign up — such as the famous poster of Lord Kitchener with the caption "Your Country Needs You".
2) Some propaganda was aimed abroad — in particular to encourage US military involvement.
3) In September 1914 the newly formed War Propaganda Bureau asked 25 of Britain's leading writers to aid the war effort. They produced pamphlets such as the Report on Alleged German Outrages (1915), which included shocking accusations of German crimes.
4) The Ministry of Information produced propaganda films, but it's not clear how much public support they generated. The propaganda film The Battle of the Somme (1916), made by The British Topical Committee, was so realistic, it could have been seen as anti-war.
5) In June 1917, the government set up a National War Aims Committee to issue propaganda literature and sponsor speeches to improve morale.

Have a propaganda at this...

This page is about people's opinions and attitudes about what happened, as well as the basic facts. Scribble a list of the main reasons why attitudes to the war changed between 1914 and 1917.

The End of the War

The war changed everybody's lives, whether they'd been away <u>fighting</u> or stayed at home. It wasn't easy to get used to <u>normal life</u> again — especially for the soldiers.

The war Finally Ended in November 1918

1) The USA entered the war in 1917. This was a massive help to the allied forces.
2) Meanwhile, trench warfare had <u>worn Germany down</u>. They <u>asked for</u> the armistice and it was signed on <u>11 November 1918</u>.
3) The peace treaty was signed at <u>Versailles</u> in <u>June 1919</u>. The conditions were harsh for Germany:

- Germany had to <u>return land</u> taken from France, Belgium, Poland and others.
- German colonies in Africa were shared between France and Britain.
- Germany had to <u>pay reparations</u> of £6600 million to compensate the Allies for the cost of the war.

The war was known as "the war to end all wars"

People in Britain thought there could <u>never</u> be another war as bad as the First World War. The <u>mood</u> in Britain immediately after the war was pretty <u>bleak</u>.

1) The government had tried to <u>control information</u> during the war. Even so, people had found out some <u>real</u> facts about the war. Many now felt that <u>politicians</u> and <u>authority figures</u> couldn't always be <u>trusted</u>.
2) Many people <u>came to believe</u> that the generals had been <u>incompetent</u>, and that they <u>didn't care</u> how many lives were lost. This gave people <u>even more reason</u> to stop trusting people in powerful positions.
3) The <u>public school officers</u> in the trenches turned out to be no more competent than the <u>working class soldiers</u>. Some people began to <u>question</u> the way the upper classes dominated society.
4) Soldiers who'd been through the war were even more <u>disillusioned</u> when they returned home. There was <u>unemployment</u> and <u>poverty</u>. They wondered what they had been <u>fighting for</u>.
5) <u>No war</u> in European history had produced so many <u>casualties</u>. It felt as though the loss of <u>huge numbers</u> of young men had changed the <u>balance of society</u>.
6) Many people in Britain were <u>very angry</u> with Germany — they wanted <u>revenge</u>. Because of this, many British people <u>supported</u> the harshness of the <u>Versailles Treaty</u>.

There were some <u>positive</u> outcomes of the war too. Even though people had many reasons to be <u>disappointed</u> there <u>was</u> a sense of satisfaction that Britain had won. Attitudes towards <u>women</u> and the <u>poorer</u> members of society generally improved, as the war showed <u>everyone</u> could do something useful if they were given the opportunity. <u>Lloyd George</u> got <u>re-elected</u> as Prime Minister in <u>December 1918</u>.

The Versailles Treaty — the roots of another war...

Don't forget the <u>final facts</u> about <u>1918</u> and the <u>Versailles Treaty</u>, as well as the <u>effects</u> of the war.

Women and the Vote

After the First World War there was a different attitude to the suffrage movement. Partly, the war had made the suffragette violence of 1913 and 1914 seem a bit less serious (p.108). But there were other reasons too — especially the work women had done for the war effort.

During the war Women did "Men's Jobs"

1) So many men were away fighting in the war that there weren't enough to do vital jobs. The jobs were opened up to women — women were happy to take them, and they proved that they could do them just as well as men.

2) Women worked as: bus conductors, drivers, postal workers, farm labourers and coal deliverers. All these vital jobs kept the country going.

3) They also worked in the munitions factories, and engineering workshops. This work was technical, and directly related to the war effort.

4) Women joined women's branches of the armed forces, and worked as nurses in military hospitals.

By doing work that helped Britain win the war, women proved they were important to public life as well as home life. There was also gratitude towards women for their contribution.

The Other Reasons for giving women the vote were...

1 A shake-up of the voting system was already happening. There was a rule that a man could only vote after living at the same address for 1 year. This needed to be changed to allow soldiers who had been away fighting to vote. If the voting system was going to be changed anyway, it was a chance to include women.

2 People's attitudes to women had changed — and not just because of the war. A lot of people remembered the suffragettes' protests and felt it was unfair that women had been denied full political rights.

3 The suffragettes had called off their campaign at the beginning of the war. Nobody wanted them starting it up again.

Women 30 and Over got the vote in 1918

1) The Representation of the People Act became law in 1918.

2) Not all women got the vote. The ones who did had to be:

over 30 and a householder	OR	married to a householder

The same Act gave all men over 21 the right to vote.

3) Women were also able to become MPs. Constance Markiewicz, a Sinn Fein candidate, was elected in 1918 but didn't take up her seat. The first woman to actually become an MP was Nancy Astor who got elected in 1919.

4) The vote didn't go to all women over 21 until 1928, when women finally got equal voting rights.

Voles for women! — sorry, I think I misread that...

The 1918 Representation of the People Act is a big landmark — make sure you know exactly which women got the vote. But just as important, scribble a list of the main reasons why they got it.

Revision Summary

Britain in 1918 was a very different place to the Britain of 1890. So many big changes, including a massive, terrible war. Such a big period in British history deserves a big load of practice questions...

1) What was the name of the institutions run to give the very poor somewhere to live and work?
2) What are the names of the two men who published reports on poverty in 1889 and 1901?
3) Which political party set up a Royal Commission to look at the Poor Law? What year was it?
4) How many reports did they write? What were they called?
5) Who won the general election in 1906?
6) Name three things children under 16 weren't allowed to do after the Children's Charter in 1908.
7) What two new ideas did Herbert Samuel come up with to help young offenders?
8) What was Part One of the National Insurance Act about?
9) What industries did Part Two of the National Insurance Act help?
10) Which two people put together the Trade Boards Act?
11) How many people got a minimum wage by 1914?
12) What were Labour Exchanges?
13) What was the popular name for Lloyd George's 1909 budget?
14) Who stopped the 1909 budget from becoming law at the first attempt?
15) Give two reasons why the Liberal reforms changed attitudes to helping the poor.
16) Give two possible jobs that a young woman could do in the 1890s.
17) Give four reasons why some people believed women shouldn't have the vote in the 1890s.
18) Who were the suffragists? Who was their leader?
19) Who were the suffragettes? In what ways were they different from the suffragists?
20) What happened in 1907 to encourage the suffragettes?
21) What happened in 1912 to make the suffragettes' campaign turn more extreme?
22) Give four examples of extreme tactics used by the suffragettes.
23) Give four things the government was allowed to do by the Defence of the Realm Act 1914.
24) When was conscription introduced?
25) What three steps did Lloyd George take to avoid a food supply crisis?
26) Give three reasons why people's attitudes to the war changed between 1914 and 1918.
27) Give two of the main points from the Versailles Treaty of 1919.
28) Give four reasons why some women got the vote after the First World War.
29) What categories of women got the right to vote in the Representation of the People Act, 1918?

How to Study History

You've learnt the facts — now you need to learn how to use them effectively. There are four key ideas that'll help you use your facts — the four 'C's: Cause, Consequence, Change, Continuity.

You'll get Questions about Causes and Consequences

1) Cause means the reason something happened — e.g. the causes of the First World War. Any time you have an event in History, think about what caused it and why it happened. There are always reasons why an event takes place and it's your job to work them out.

2) Consequence means what happened because of an action — it's the result of an event, e.g. a consequence of the Second World War was that the USA and USSR became superpowers because the big powers in Europe had become very weak.

> 1) Some questions will ask you to give an opinion about causes and consequences — e.g. "'The failure of the League of Nations was caused by the Great Depression.' How far do you agree with this statement?" or "What do you think were the most important effects of glasnost and perestroika?".
>
> 2) It's up to you what opinion you give — but you've got to be able to back it up with reasons and facts.
>
> 3) With this type of question, it's good to mention several causes /consequences — and then explain which you think was the most important and why.

You also need to think about Change and Continuity

1) Change is when something happens to make things different — there can be quick changes, e.g. the assassination of Archduke Franz Ferdinand contributed to the outbreak of the First World War. Or there can be slow changes, e.g. the tensions between Britain and Germany in the early 1900s were a long-term factor leading to the start of the First World War.

2) Continuity is the opposite of change — it means when things stay the same, e.g. Tsar Nicholas II's dynasty ruled Russia for 300 years.

3) These ideas are opposites — think of continuity as a flat line going along until there is a sudden change and the line becomes a zigzag:

> Use the four 'C's in your answers — link facts together and tell the examiners why something happened and what the results were. Explain if there was a change and if so, what things changed from and what they changed to.

Time for some exam tips...

Obviously, you're going to need to learn all the info for your topics. But to get high marks, you need to do more than just trot out the facts. You need to be able to discuss topics in a thoughtful way, showing good understanding. The four 'C's are really useful for this.

Handling Sources

There are few certainties in life — but you will get <u>source questions</u> in your exam...

There are Two Main Kinds of Sources

1) <u>Primary sources</u> — this is evidence <u>from</u> the period you're studying, e.g. a newspaper report on the First World War from 4th September 1914.

2) <u>Secondary sources</u> — this is evidence <u>about</u> a historical period, e.g. a 1989 book entitled 'Origins of the First World War'.

    Sources may be <u>visual extracts</u>, e.g. photographs and maps, or <u>written extracts</u>, e.g. diaries, newspapers etc.

If You Want to Do Well Look at Sources Carefully

1) You've got to find <u>evidence</u> from the source which is <u>relevant</u> to the question.
2) Show you <u>understand</u> the source, and use the facts you already know about the period to <u>explain</u> what the source is saying, and <u>how</u> it says it.
3) Say <u>how reliable and useful</u> you think the source is. Think about whether the source gives <u>enough</u> information about the topic or if there are <u>gaps</u> or <u>inconsistencies</u>. Say if you think the source is <u>biased</u> (one-sided in its opinions) — and if so, why.

> Don't confuse facts and opinions — always think about <u>who</u> is writing, <u>why</u> they are writing and <u>what</u> they are trying to say.

Top Tips for Answering Source Questions

Do

1) <u>Use</u> the source material to help answer the question — don't just rely on what you know already.
2) Check what the source tells you — look out for <u>what</u> a source says, <u>who</u> wrote it and <u>when</u> they wrote it.
3) <u>Read</u> the question <u>carefully</u>. E.g. if it says to use three sources A, B and C, you must use all three.
4) If you're asked to look at more than one source, then <u>compare them</u>.
5) Use the <u>facts you already know</u> about the period to <u>help you understand</u> the source and judge how useful it is.

Don't

1) Don't get carried away writing down everything you know about the topic — <u>focus</u> on the source(s) given.
2) <u>Don't jump to conclusions</u> — e.g. don't assume that every eyewitness account is accurate.
3) <u>Don't</u> always take sources at <u>face value</u>. E.g. a history book about the Russian Revolution that was written in Stalin's USSR might <u>exaggerate</u> his role and <u>leave out</u> people like Trotsky.

Historians love ketchup — they're obsessed with sources...

Evaluating sources is an <u>important skill</u> for historians — and one you have to demonstrate in the exam. So if you want decent grades, put the effort into learning this page right now.

Exam Essay Skills

You've also got to be able to tackle <u>essay answers</u>...

Planning *Your Exam Time*

1) On the exam paper, it'll say next to each question <u>how many marks</u> it's worth.
2) Look out for which questions have <u>most marks</u> — make sure you spend <u>most time</u> on these.
3) There'll be at least one or two questions which require <u>essay-length</u> answers.

> <u>Learn the rule</u> — the <u>more marks</u> a question is worth, the <u>longer</u> your answer should be. Don't get carried away writing loads for a question that's only worth 4 marks — you need to <u>leave time</u> for the higher mark questions.

Remember these *Three Tips* for writing good *Essays*

1) Plan your Essay

<u>Sort out</u> what you want to say before you start writing — think about <u>how to answer the question</u>, and what the <u>key words</u> are. Scribble a <u>quick plan</u> of your main points — <u>cross through this neatly</u> at the end, so it's obvious it shouldn't be marked.

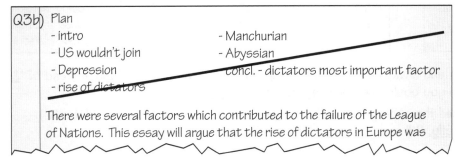

Q3b) Plan
- intro   - Manchurian
- US wouldn't join   - Abyssian
- Depression   concl. - dictators most important factor
- rise of dictators

There were several factors which contributed to the failure of the League of Nations. This essay will argue that the rise of dictators in Europe was

2) Stay Focused *on the Question*

Make sure that you <u>directly answer the question</u>. <u>Back up your points</u> with relevant facts. Don't just chuck in everything you know. You've got to be <u>relevant</u> and <u>accurate</u> — e.g. if you're writing about the rise of the Nazi Party, don't include stories about a London camel called George who moved rubble during the Blitz.

3) Use a Clear *Writing Style*

Your essay should start with a brief <u>introduction</u> and end with a <u>conclusion</u>. Remember to start a <u>new paragraph</u> for each new point you want to discuss. Try to use <u>clear handwriting</u> — and pay attention to <u>spelling</u>, <u>grammar</u> and <u>punctuation</u> (see p.118-121).

1) introduction
2) content
3) conclusion

There's no need to panic in the exam...

Even if you've revised properly, remembered a spare pen and arrived early for your exam, there's a chance you'll suffer from 'mind blank syndrome' when you open the paper. But don't panic, just stay calm, <u>read the questions carefully</u>, and <u>use the advice</u> you've learnt here. Good luck.

Spelling, Punctuation and Grammar

You get marks in your exams for having good <u>SPaG</u> (spelling, punctuation and grammar). This stuff might not be particularly thrilling but if you can get it right, it's <u>easy marks</u>. This page is about checking your work...

Remember *to Check* what you've Written

1) Leave <u>5 minutes</u> at the end of the exam to <u>check your work</u>.

2) 5 minutes <u>isn't</u> long, so there <u>won't</u> be time to check <u>everything</u> thoroughly. Look for the <u>most obvious</u> spelling, punctuation and grammar <u>mistakes</u>.

3) <u>Start</u> by checking your answers to the questions which award <u>SPaG marks</u>. There'll be instructions on the exam paper telling you which these are. <u>Only</u> check the rest of your answers if you've got <u>time</u>.

Check for common *Spelling Mistakes*

When you're writing under pressure, it's <u>easy</u> to let <u>spelling mistakes</u> creep in, but there are a few things you can watch out for:

Check for missing words as well as misspelt words.

1) Look out for words which <u>sound the same</u> but <u>mean different things</u> and are <u>spelt differently</u>. Make sure you've used the correct one. For example, 'their', 'they're' and 'there':

Woodrow Wilson thought colonies should have say in <u>their</u> own future.	East Germany and West Germany were divided for 45 years, but now <u>they're</u> one country again.	Under Tsar Nicholas II <u>there</u> were food shortages, demonstrations and strikes.

2) <u>Don't</u> use text speak, and always write words out <u>in full</u>. For example, use '<u>and</u>' instead of '<u>&</u>' or '<u>+</u>'. <u>Don't</u> use '<u>etc.</u>' when you could give <u>more examples</u> or a <u>better explanation</u>.

3) Make sure you've used the appropriate <u>technical terms</u> (like 'collectivisation' or 'détente'). If they're <u>spelt correctly</u>, it'll really <u>impress</u> the <u>examiner</u>.

Make sure your *Grammar* and *Punctuation* are *Correct*

1) Check you've used <u>capital letters</u>, <u>full stops</u> and <u>question marks</u> correctly (see p.121).

2) Make sure your writing <u>isn't too chatty</u> and doesn't use <u>slang words</u>. It should be <u>formal</u>.

3) Watch out for sentences where your writing switches between <u>different tenses</u>. You should usually stick to <u>one tense</u> throughout your answer (don't worry if you quote from a source that's in a different tense).

4) Check that you've started a <u>new paragraph</u> every time you make a new point. It's important that your answer <u>isn't</u> just <u>one long block</u> of text (see p.121).

5) Watch out for tricksy little <u>grammar mistakes</u>:

   • Remember — '<u>it's</u>' (with an apostrophe) is short for '<u>it is</u>' or '<u>it has</u>'. '<u>Its</u>' (without an apostrophe) means '<u>belonging to it</u>'.

   • It's always '<u>should have</u>', not 'should of' (the same goes for 'could have' and 'would have' too).

   If you know that you <u>often</u> confuse two words, like 'it's' and 'its', <u>watch out</u> for them when you're checking your work in the exam.

Check, check, check, goose, check, check, check...

Blimey, there's a lot of stuff to check... which is why it's really important to practise it all <u>before</u> the exam. That way it'll be second nature, so you'll do it all automatically and make <u>fewer errors</u> in the first place.

Spelling, Punctuation and Grammar

Making a mistake in your exam is <u>not</u> the end of the world, so don't panic if you find one.
If you just cross it out <u>neatly</u> and correct the mistake, you <u>won't</u> lose any marks at all — excellent.

Make your corrections Neatly

1) If the mistake is just <u>one word</u> or a <u>short phrase</u>, cross it out <u>neatly</u> and write the correct word <u>above</u> it.

> Communist party members loyal to Stalin ~~recieved~~ ^{received} privileges such as holidays.

2) If you've <u>forgotten</u> to start a <u>new paragraph</u>, use a <u>double strike</u>
(like this '//') to show where the new paragraph should <u>begin</u>:

See p.121 for more on paragraphs.

> Collectivisation helped peasants work together and provided large-scale organisation
> for food production. **//** However, the new system was not very successful at first.
> Many people died of starvation after a bad harvest caused a serious famine, which was
> made worse by the kulaks, who had started to destroy crops and animals in protest.

If only someone had told Graham about the double strike.

Use an Asterisk to add Extra Information

1) If you've <u>missed something out</u>, think about whether you have space to write the missing bit <u>above</u>
the line you've already written. If you <u>can</u>, use a ' ∧ ' to show <u>exactly where</u> it should go.

> Civil rights issues became a particular focus in 1955, with the Montgomery bus boycott.
> Rosa Parks was arrested for refusing to give up her bus seat for a white man. Martin
> Luther King reacted by organising a ^{bus}∧boycott with other black ministers. The success
> of their peaceful protest was inspirational to everyone who opposed segregation.

2) If the bit you've missed out <u>won't</u> fit above the line, use an <u>asterisk</u> (like this '*') to show the examiner
<u>where</u> the missing bit should go.

3) Write the <u>missing words</u> at the <u>end</u> of your answer with another asterisk next to them.

> The Treaty of Versailles was very harsh on Germany. A lot of land[*] was confiscated
> and Germany was forced by Article 231 to accept the blame for the war.
>   * including Alsace and Lorraine

Cross Out anything you Don't want to be Marked

1) If you've written something that you <u>don't</u> want the examiner to mark, <u>cross it out neatly</u>.
2) Cross out any <u>notes</u>. If you don't <u>finish</u> your answer <u>in time</u>, don't cross out your <u>plan</u> —
the examiner might look at it to see what you were <u>going to write</u>.
3) Don't <u>scribble things out</u> without thinking — it'll make your answers look <u>messy</u>.

When making corrections, neatness is the name of ^{the}∧game

Examiners love it if your answer is <u>neat</u> and <u>tidy</u> — it makes it super easy for them to read. This means they
can spend more time giving you lots of <u>marks</u> for the great stuff you've written. So neatness is win-win.

Spelling, Punctuation and Grammar

Some words are darn tricky to spell. The only way to be sure you'll get them right is to <u>learn</u> them <u>off by heart</u>. This page has some of the <u>most common</u> ones you'll need to know for your history exams.

Learn these *Useful Words*

The underlined words are useful in a lot of <u>answers</u>, so you need to know <u>how</u> to <u>spell</u> them.

> There are convincing <u>arguments</u> for and against Haig's tactics in World War One.

> The Nazis were <u>successful</u> at controlling people through fear and propaganda.

> Chamberlain signed the Munich Agreement <u>because</u> he <u>believed</u> Hitler would keep his promises.

> Fidel Castro <u>attempted</u> to overthrow Batista.

> The Wall Street Crash <u>affected</u> companies across the world.

> American banks were <u>encouraged</u> to lend money to lots of <u>businesses</u> in the 1920s.

> There are many <u>differences</u> between the New Economic Policy and War Communism.

Spell *Technical Words* Correctly

There are a lot of <u>technical words</u> in History. You need to be able to <u>spell</u> them <u>correctly</u>. <u>Learn</u> these examples to start you off. The <u>coloured letters</u> are the tricky bits to watch out for.

agriculture	constitution	evidence	parliament
alliance	defence	fascism	rebellion
biased	democracy	foreign	reliability
conflict	diplomacy	league	resistance
controversial	effective	military	source

You'll also have to learn how to spell the names and technical terms from the options you're studying. So for Germany 1918-45 you'll need to be comfortable with names like 'Stresemann' and terms such as 'the Luftwaffe'. Go back through the options you've studied and make a list of all the tricky names and words you'll need — then get them learnt.

Learn this page and make spelling errors history...

Mnemonics can help you remember how to spell tricky words. For example, you can remember 'biased' with the phrase '<u>B</u>ecause <u>I</u> <u>A</u>dore <u>S</u>ugary, <u>E</u>nglish <u>D</u>oughnuts' or '<u>B</u>leary <u>I</u>nsomniacs <u>A</u>void <u>S</u>leep <u>E</u>very <u>D</u>ay'.

Spelling, Punctuation and Grammar

This page is full of tips for good <u>punctuation</u> and <u>grammar</u> to help you avoid making any silly mistakes, hurrah!

You need to Punctuate Properly...

1) Always use a <u>capital letter</u> at the start of a <u>sentence</u>.
   Use capital letters for <u>names</u> of <u>particular people</u>, <u>places</u> and <u>things</u>. For example:

   All sentences start with capital letters. → <u>I</u>n 1933 <u>H</u>itler was made <u>C</u>hancellor of <u>G</u>ermany.

   The name of a person.   A title.   The name of a country.

2) <u>Full stops</u> go at the end of <u>sentences</u>, e.g. 'Archduke Franz Ferdinand was killed in June 1914<u>.</u>'
   <u>Question marks</u> go at the end of <u>questions</u>, e.g. 'How successful was the New Deal<u>?</u>'

3) Use <u>commas</u> when you use <u>more than one adjective</u> to describe something, or to separate items in a <u>list</u>:

   > Hitler envisioned a <u>highly militarised</u>, <u>racially superior</u> German nation.

   > Lenin's April Theses promised <u>peace</u>, <u>bread</u>, <u>land</u> and freedom.

4) <u>Commas</u> can also <u>join two points</u> into one sentence with a joining word (such as '<u>and</u>', '<u>or</u>', '<u>so</u>' or '<u>but</u>'):

   > Old Communist leaders opposed change, <u>so</u> they decided to get rid of Gorbachev.

   > Hoover tried to help big business, <u>but</u> he didn't do enough to help ordinary people.

5) <u>Commas</u> can also be used to separate <u>extra information</u> in a sentence:

   > Gorbachev, <u>who became General Secretary of the Communist Party in 1985</u>, was more open to the West than previous leaders.

   > David Lloyd George, <u>leader of the Liberal Party</u>, pushed for social reforms to help the poor.

   When you use commas like this, the sentence should still make sense when the extra bit is taken out.

...and use Grammar Correctly

1) <u>Don't change tenses</u> in your writing by mistake:

   > Some business people were angry that the New Deal allowed trade unions into the workplace.

   <u>Both</u> verbs are in the <u>past tense</u> — which is correct. Writing '<u>allows</u>' instead of '<u>allowed</u>' would be wrong.

2) <u>Don't</u> use <u>double negatives</u>. You should only use a negative <u>once</u> in a sentence:

   > It was called the Cold War because there wasn't any direct fighting.   Don't put 'no' here.

3) Write your longer answers in <u>paragraphs</u>. A paragraph is a <u>group of sentences</u> which talk about the <u>same thing</u> or <u>follow on</u> from each other. You need to start a <u>new paragraph</u> when you start making a <u>new point</u>. You show a <u>new paragraph</u> by starting a <u>new line</u> and leaving a <u>gap</u> (an <u>indent</u>) before you start writing:

   This gap shows a new paragraph. →
   > From 1933 Hitler started a programme of public works, such as the building of huge new motorways. This gave jobs to thousands of people.
   >   Even though there was increased employment, the Nazis altered the statistics so that things looked better than they were. Wages were also poor.

   When you <u>plan</u> long answers, remember that you should write a <u>new paragraph</u> for each of your main points.

Phew, now you're fully SPaG-ed and ready to go...

Having good SPaG is a great way to get <u>marks</u> in the exam, and having bad SPaG is a great way to lose marks. Which is why it's dead <u>important</u> to learn all the stuff on this page (and all the other pages too).

Index